Basic Skills Support

A Guide for Every Teacher

by Sue Silk

ALBSU
Registered Charity No. 1003059

The Basic Skills Unit

Acknowledgements

In writing this publication I have drawn together a lot of the work that has been developed during the ALBSU Special Development Project at Wakefield College. Other colleagues from within the College have also been generous in sharing their work. These include: Chris Maples, Clare Macdonald, Deirdre Twomey, Chris Hopwood, Christine Clements, Cynthia Day, Judy Rylance, Sue Elliott, Melanie Allen, Kathy Seacome, Joyce Simmons and Helen Chater.

I would also like to thank Henry Kelly of South Tyneside College and Derek Newton from City of Liverpool College for their help with some of the details about numeracy support work.

A very special thanks also to Karen Town for her patience and good humour in typing this publication.

Published October 1994

ISBN 1 85990 009 7

Design: Studio 21

Contents

1 | *Introducing Basic Skills Support*

- What is basic skills support?
- Who needs basic skills support?
- Why is support needed?
- Funding for F.E.
- National Targets for Education and Training
- Targets for increased participation in F.E.
- National Qualifications Framework

This chapter defines basic skills support for the purposes of this book. It also outlines some of the factors that have influenced this development and sets basic skills support into context within a rapidly changing further education sector.

What is basic skills support?

Basic skills support is concerned with helping students to improve their basic skills in order that they are able to progress and achieve a successful outcome on their vocational or academic course. It is provided as part of some other education or training provision.

By basic skills ALBSU means:

> *"the ability to read, write and speak English and use mathematics at a level necessary to function and progress at work and in society in general."*

The provision of literacy, numeracy and English for Speakers of Other Languages (ESOL) is included in this definition of basic skills. In Wales, basic skills includes the ability to read and write Welsh for people whose first language is Welsh.

Basic skills support is part of a wide range of support services that are usually available to students. These include:

- **Personal Counselling**
- **Educational and Careers Guidance**
- **Learning Resource Centres**
- **Financial Advice**
- **Childcare Facilities.**

It is distinct from the provision that is available for students with learning disabilities or other identified special needs.

Who needs basic skills support?

Many students, on a wide range of college courses at all levels, will experience difficulties and seek help with particular aspects of basic skills at some time in their course. They may require a short input or a more sustained programme of work throughout their course to develop the skills and competences that they require. Many more students will continue to struggle with course work and assignments. Some may leave the course or fail to achieve at the end of it.

In May 1994 ALBSU conducted a survey of just under 150 colleges who had used the screening tool published as *Assessing Reading and Maths.* Of this total 126 colleges excluded students with learning difficulties and/or disabilities and students in primary basic skills provision from screening. Most colleges screened only selected groups of students, from courses where basic skills support needs were experienced or anticipated.

The results indicate levels of need as follows:

Reading

Below Foundation	1% of all students	will need support to achieve NVQ even at Level 1
Foundation	11%	
Level 1	18%	may need support to achieve NVQ at Level 2 and above
Above Level 1	69%	

Numeracy

Below Foundation	2%	will need support to achieve NVQ even at Level 1
Foundation	12%	
Level 1	30%	may need support to achieve NVQ at Level 2 and above
Above Level 1	57%	

These underpinning communication and numerical skills, tested in the screening, are essential to ensure the successful completion of courses. They are the foundation from which individuals will progress within education, work and everyday life.

Why is support needed?

The question is often asked: "Why should students entering further education still need basic skills development?"

The reasons are many and varied:

- Further education is a second chance for many students who were poorly motivated at school. Students who underachieved in key areas of the curriculum, especially English and maths, find that they will need to develop these skills in order to progress within their chosen vocational area.

- Frequent illness or absence has interrupted previous educational experience and may have left significant gaps in the student's knowledge.

- A time lapse between leaving school and entering further education means that basic skills need to be revised and developed.

- Different delivery methods on courses place increasing responsibility on students for their own learning. Often these demand high levels of literacy, numeracy and language.

- Basic skills need to be applied within the vocational context and students can find this difficult, particularly with numeracy skills.

- Vocationally related texts may be written in an unfamiliar register and concepts and ideas may be expressed using vocabulary and language structures that are new to the student. If students find it difficult to get to grips with the language aspects of a course, their progress will be hindered.

- Evidence of core skills competence is a requirement on an increasing number of courses. This applies to all GNVQ courses. It is possible that this will be extended to include other courses within the post-16 sector and students may be expected to undertake a programme of development in the key areas of Communications, Application of Number and IT.

- Students may have some vocational experience and competence but lack the necessary language skills to gain qualifications in this country. An intensive programme of language support within the vocational context may speed up progress.

These are the factors influencing the individual student but, further education as a whole is at the forefront of rapid change. A number of external factors are shaping the development of education and training.

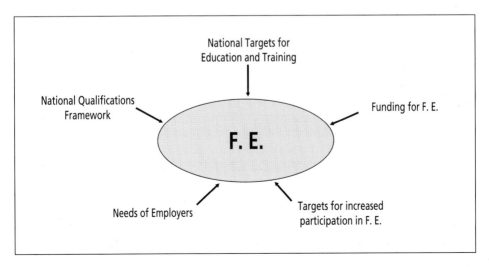

Funding for F.E.

Further Education Colleges are now funded through two Further Education Funding Councils; one for England and one for Wales. Funding will be based on units rather than enrolments and each student will attract a number of units. Colleges will be funded for three main elements:

- **on-entry recruitment activities**

- **on-programme learning activities**

- **student achievement/attainment.**

A percentage of the funding is attached to each of these elements. The largest proportion is for on-programme activities. Colleges will only be able to claim all the units of funding if students stay on a course and achieve a positive outcome, usually a qualification, at the end. In England funding will also be available for additional support for students who need extra literacy, numeracy or ESOL tuition in order to complete the course. Counselling and guidance on-entry will be a key part in this process and a significant factor in this will be the effective assessment of students' basic skills. On-programme support for basic skills can then be tailored to suit the needs of groups or individuals. This will be vital if retention and achievement rates are to be improved.

National Targets for Education and Training (NTETs)

National targets have been set by the government for both young people and adults in the workforce which are aimed at increasing the number of people achieving qualifications within the national vocational qualifications framework at NVQ Level II and NVQ Level III. It is likely that these targets will be revised in line with developments in Europe and other parts of the world. They may include targets for improving basic skills. The role of core skills within the whole qualifications framework is expanding and developing, further supporting the necessity for well developed basic skills.

Targets for increased participation in F.E.

The expansion of the further education sector means that many new students will be recruited from sections of the community who have not traditionally participated in education. Adults will increasingly be drawn into further education and training, either as part of their training commitment as an employee or in an effort to update existing skills or learn new ones. In many areas, traditional occupations are in decline and different industries are developing that require new skills. New technology, health and safety requirements and the need for flexibility means that people will be required to transfer their skills into new contexts. Women, students from ethnic minorities and the long term unemployed are being encouraged into education and training. In order to realise their potential, many may need to develop their basic skills or build their confidence within the context of their course and sometimes in addition to it. Open access policies mean that colleges will have to develop systems for the assessment of students' basic skills and provision that is flexible and vocationally-related to meet the demand for increased competence in communications, numeracy and IT.

Needs of Employers

The cost to industry of poor basic skills is estimated at £4.8 billion per year. The cost to the individuals involved is also high, resulting in a lack of opportunity to progress at work or to develop the new skills necessary for particular jobs. Companies repeatedly highlight the poor basic skills of the workforce or prospective workforce, including those who are recently qualified. The responsibility for this does not lie solely with colleges, but they have a significant part to play, not least in ensuring that students have the opportunity to develop their basic skills as part of their educational entitlement.

> *"The top slice of output is excellent by international standards; the bulk of the remainder is not. The weaknesses are in basic literacy and numeracy and in the limited level of vocational training."*
>
> GKN reporting to the Trade and Industry Committee – April 1994

The U.K. needs a well educated and well trained workforce. Competence in a range of basic skills has become more important, particularly with changing work organisation and the impact of information technology on working practices. Further education has a vital role to play in the development of work related basic skills.

National Qualifications Framework

Recent developments, notably the National Vocational Qualifications framework, have accelerated changes in the ways that courses are delivered and in the roles of both tutors and students. The core skills of Communication, Application of Number and IT are already an integral part of GNVQ courses. Students are expected to take an active role in directing their learning and organising evidence of this learning. Resource based learning will play an increasing part in the delivery of courses. Students who lack the underpinning basic skills will find great difficulty with this type of delivery and as a result may lack confidence and underachieve in many areas of their course.

Many college staff expect that students will have these skills already when they enrol on the course. This assumption can lead to students' needs going unrecognised with the danger that the students will have left the course before positive action can be taken. This is to the detriment of both the individual and the institution.

The discovery of the amount of basic numeracy and communication skills needed to pass vocational courses can come as a shock to students who often perceive these courses as practically based. Course information and counselling pre-enrolment has an important function in informing students about all aspects of the course including basic skills.

Within all these changes, the student remains as the central focus and their development within their chosen field, the central aim. However different the demands of each curriculum area are, it is clear that students will need the underpinning skills of literacy, numeracy and language in order to function and develop effectively. A proportion of students will not have sufficiently developed these skills before entering further education, so ways of identifying their needs and supporting them are of crucial importance. Colleges will need to have policies, provision and staff development programmes in place to facilitate this so that poorly developed basic skills are not a barrier to progress in further education and training.

2 | *Assessing the need for Basic Skills Support*

This chapter will look at basic skills screening and explore some of the issues about when to screen and whether to use a generic screening or a course specific assessment.

There are several fundamental questions to be asked before a college decides when and how screening should be done;

- **What are the expectations of the College in terms of the information they expect to gain from the screening, and how will this information be used?**

- **Is it to be used post-enrolment to determine which students will need communication, numeracy or second language support?**

- **Is it expected that screening will form part of the on-entry information about a students and be used as a basis from which learning gain can be measured?**

- **Who is the screening information for: vocational tutors, basic skills support tutors or both?**

- **Is it a way of providing information about students with few formal educational qualifications?**

The answers to these questions will determine which screening method is used and how this is followed through with further assessment and monitoring.

Screening is a useful tool but not an infallible indicator and on its own may not provide all the information necessary to make an informed judgement about a student's current functioning level or a prediction of their likely future performance.

Why use screening?

- **to assess the current level of a student**

- **to identify the needs of individual students and particular groups of students**

11

- **to target support efficiently and appropriately**

- **to improve retention rates.**

Screening can be done in a number of ways. Students can have their performance assessed against objective criteria as in the ALBSU 'Assessing Reading and Maths', they can be interviewed and counselled by college staff and they can be given assessment tasks which are then judged by the course team against their expectations of the skills students will have coming onto a particular programme. Students can be given self assessment checklists, for example, on their enrolment form. Involving students in some way in this assessment process is important so that they can begin to become aware of their own abilities in relation to the course that they are on. However, students do not always have a realistic view of their own abilities. Often a variety of screening and assessment methods are used.

Basic skills screening is aimed at:

- **identifying quickly those students whose level of competence falls below certain criteria**

It is useful for:

- **identifying individuals and groups of students whose literacy and/or numeracy is at a level below which it is reasonable to expect them to be able to function effectively and progress on their course**
- **building up a cross-college picture of need will help to identify the level of resources needed to establish and develop provision**
- **opening up a dialogue with vocational staff about the needs of students and ways of supporting them.**

It is intended to be a supportive process for students in that it provides staff with an 'early warning system' which forms the basis of further observation and assessment. **It is only the beginning of the assessment process.** It is not intended that screening should be used to exclude students from programmes.

To be effective, screening needs to be part of a well organised system aimed at providing students with a relevant learning programme during their time in college. The point at which the screening is administered is dependent on the organisation of initial advice and guidance procedures as well as the length and purpose of the induction period. A common induction period that is used to both inform students of their options and give staff the opportunity to assess the students skills before finally negotiating the learning programme would include screening for literacy and numeracy as part of the assessment activities.

Screening forms only part of the information that is known about students. Previous achievements at school, employment experience, as well as their personal attitudes and motivation all contribute to their ability to succeed on a course. A lot of this information will not, however, be in a form that enables a learning plan for individual students to be developed easily. A GCSE grade can give an idea of the range of skills that students might have acquired but does not differentiate clearly where there are weaknesses. It will not give any indication of a student's ability to apply these skills in the vocational context.

When to screen

Looking at the processes that take place before the full on-programme activities commence shows that screening for basic skills can take place at a number of points in the process.

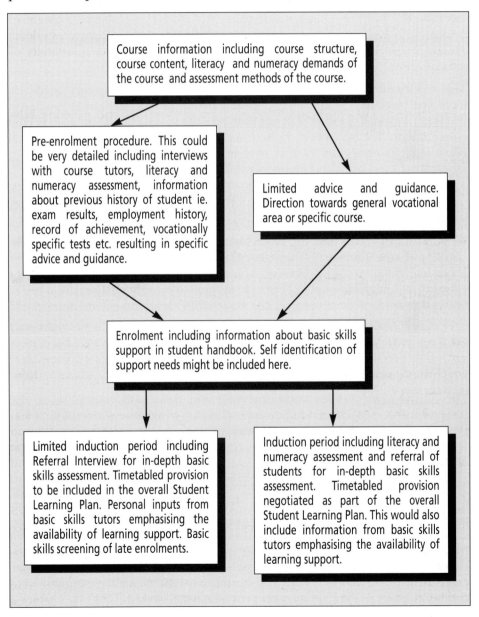

The key factors in any system are:

- **the quality of the course information in giving students a holistic view of all the skills needed on the course**

- **the awareness of advice and guidance staff and vocational staff of the literacy, language and numeracy demands of courses**

- **the inclusion of information about basic skills support in student and staff handbooks**

- **the further assessment of students who need additional support by basic skills staff**

- **the timetabling of support provision in the overall Student Learning Plan.**

This will ensure that those students who have significant support needs are identified immediately and enable colleges to apply for additional funding if this is appropriate. Support will not then be seen by students as an unexpected commitment that has been 'bolted on' to the college programme. It will become an integral part of that student's course and the whole process of monitoring attendance and progress will be part of the mainstream activity.

This is a change in emphasis from the approaches used in the past which relied on self referral and voluntary attendance at classes and workshops. This was not necessarily seen as part of the college course. The effects of modularisation on college timetables and the Accreditation of Prior Learning mean that the concept of an individually negotiated timetable is a reality, with students accessing modules of provision according to their need and previous educational and vocational experience. Systems for credit accumulation are in the early stages of development and basic skills development modules could support this type of structure.

Organising screening

The involvement of both vocational staff and basic skills specialists in the screening process is of vital importance. Creating a dialogue with course tutors throughout the College at the beginning of the year by involving them in the administration and marking of the screening can alert those tutors to the needs of their student group.

The assessment of students' skills is the responsibility of all staff although some may have a more specialised role than others in implementing support strategies. Screening can provide course tutors with valuable insights into students' difficulties with areas of the course. Poor motivation, disruptive behaviour and lack of understanding can often be traced to a basic skills problem. Screening often alerts staff to potential problems or supports earlier assessment of the student. Staff responsible for basic skills need to also have this information so that the relevant provision is developed.

The ALBSU screening takes twenty minutes in all to complete. It has two cloze passages to assess reading, one at Foundation Level and the other at Level 1 of the ALBSU Standards. It has two numeracy sections, one requiring students to have skills at Foundation Level and the other at Level 1 of the ALBSU Standards.

READING ASSESSMENT

Safe as houses?

SECTION B

We think of our home as a safe place to be, and are more worried when someone goes out of the house than when they stay at home. In fact (1)_____ people die from accidents in (2)_____ home every year than are (3)_____ on roads or at work.

(4)_____ are the causes of these (5)_____ in the home? Many people may (6)_____ of fire as the greatest (7)_____, but in fact more people (8)_____ from falling than from any (9)_____ cause. Tragic accidents, some fatal, (10)_____ caused by children and adults (11)_____, walking, or falling through glass (12)_____ and windows. Poisoning can also (13)_____ illness or death. This may (14)_____ from medicines or from household substances (15)_____ as cleaning materials. Food (16)_____ is also a common danger.

Statistics (17)_____ that most accidents happen on Mondays (18)_____ at weekends. People are at work (19)_____ now and have more leisure (20)_____. They therefore spend more time (21)_____ home. This has led to (22)_____ increase in the number of (23)_____ in the home. The two (24)_____ vulnerable groups of people (25)_____ young children (especially pre-school (26)_____) and the elderly. These groups (27)_____ more time in the home (28)_____, for example, older children who (29)_____ at school, or adults (30)_____ are out at work during the (31)_____. The elderly are weaker and (32)_____ slower reactions. Young children are (33)_____ aware of the dangers in (34)_____ home, and are dependent on (35)_____ carers being aware of dangerous (36)_____.

Total

Total: 36 marks

This is the end of the Reading Assessment. Go on to the next page when you are told to.

It identifies students' skills in reading and numeracy as being below, at or above these levels. Further assessment can then be carried out immediately on individual students with low scores, in reading and/or numeracy, in relation to

NUMERACY ASSESSMENT

SECTION B

Answers

1. You need to buy some coffee. The shop has the following offers:
    a) 50 grams   £0.75   c) 200 grams £2.49
    b) 400 grams £5.13   d) 100 grams £1.39

    Which is the best buy?

2. You are decorating your room and need some new tools.
    You buy: A 13 mm paint brush   £1.48
              A 38 mm paint brush   £3.52
              A paint roller set   £3.29
              Sandpaper   £1.45

    How much have you spent?

3. A tin of paint costs £8.00.
    There is 10% discount on all goods bought today.

    How much discount do you get off the paint?

4. You spend £13.56 on groceries and give in £20.00.
    How much change do you get back?

5. These figures show the number of people visiting the local cinema in the last 2 months.

    a) Round the figures up or   January 15,600
       down to the nearest 1,000.
                                          February 17,250

    b) Complete the bar
       chart using these
       figures.
       April   15,000
       May   12,000
       June   14,000
       July   13,000
       August   11,000

    | 15,000 |
    | 14,000 |
    | 13,000 |
    | 12,000 |
    | 11,000 |
    | 10,000 |

    April   May   June   July   August

6. ¾ of passengers travelling on the London train have got reduced fare tickets. There are 200 passengers on the train.

    How many have full price tickets?

Total

End of assessment

Total: 7 marks

16

the level of course that they are on. The ALBSU screening does not assess a students' ability to compose and execute a piece of writing.

A generic screening assessment such as ALBSU *Assessing Reading and Maths'* can be organised in the following way.

Administration and follow-up of screening

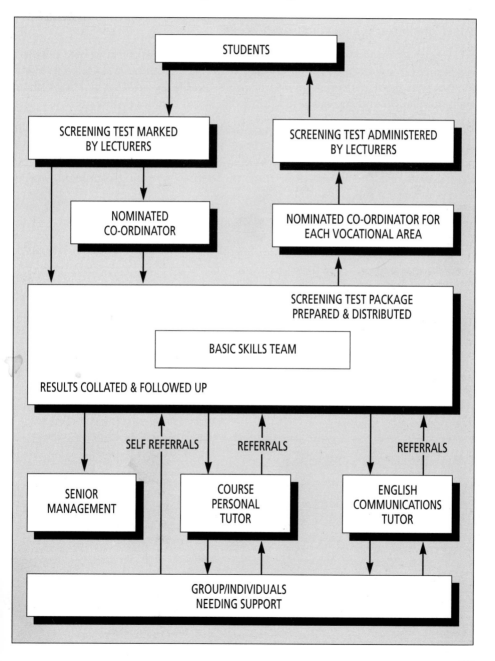

Creating links between basic skills staff and vocational areas enables referral and further assessment to take place more easily, particularly if clear information is given to staff about referring students and some training has been done that assists staff in interpreting the screening results. Individual students who are likely to need help can then be followed up quickly.

Should the same screening be used across the college or should it be specific to courses or vocational areas?

Screening is intended to be a relatively fast process with more detailed assessment being done at the next stage with those students who need it. Many factors will need to be taken into account about the student not least their own motivation and background knowledge about the vocational area.

Course specific assessments often take longer to administer and mark and all students are scrutinised in more detail at this stage. Students who need additional support for basic skills will then need to have an Individual Learning Plan drawn up. The information from the course specific assessment would form the basis of this.

There are a number of advantages and disadvantages for both methods.

GENERIC SCREENING	
ADVANTAGES	**DISADVANTAGES**
• provides a whole college approach	• not vocationally related
• quick and easy to administer	• gives limited information in relation to specific areas of the course
• gives figures that are easily collated	• may only concentrate on the lower levels
• provides a cross-college picture	• further assessment activities need to be undertaken before an individual learning plan can be drawn up
• relates to the same set of objective criteria	
• can be marked by non-specialists	

COURSE SPECIFIC ASSESSMENT	
ADVANTAGES	**DISADVANTAGES**
• related to the skills profile of the course	• more difficult to build a cross college picture
• tutors who may have collaborated in its development will have ownership. Course tutors can become more easily involved in the support of students	• needs considerable development time
	• more time consuming to administer and mark
• may assess a wider range of skills	• may vary in its effectiveness from course to course
• may offer more useful information that will form the basis of diagnostic assessment that can be used for an individual learning plan	• less easy to define objective criteria against which to devise and mark the assessment
	• relies more on the skills of tutors who are devising and marking the assessments
	• subjective elements may well creep into the marking
	• may not be clear about the level of skills and specialist knowledge that students are expected to have at the start of the course.
	• needs specialised skills to develop that may not be possessed by all staff

What conclusions can be drawn from screening?

Screening can raise the awareness of need within the college for student support. It can influence the decisions that are made. In this way an infrastructure is built within an institution that supports staff and students.

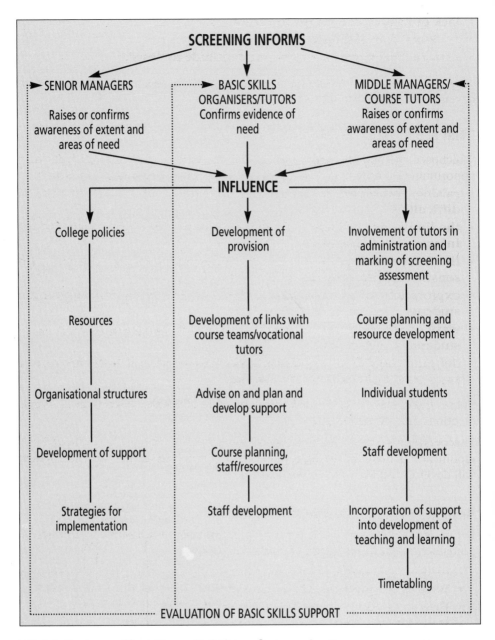

SCREENING INFORMS

SENIOR MANAGERS
Raises or confirms awareness of extent and areas of need

BASIC SKILLS ORGANISERS/TUTORS
Confirms evidence of need

MIDDLE MANAGERS/ COURSE TUTORS
Raises or confirms awareness of extent and areas of need

INFLUENCE

College policies

Development of provision

Involvement of tutors in administration and marking of screening assessment

Resources

Development of links with course teams/vocational tutors

Course planning and resource development

Organisational structures

Advise on and plan and develop support

Individual students

Development of support

Course planning, staff/resources

Staff development

Strategies for implementation

Staff development

Incorporation of support into development of teaching and learning

Timetabling

EVALUATION OF BASIC SKILLS SUPPORT

Which factors affect the reliability of screening?

A screening tool is not only limited by the range and level of skills that it can cover, but also by other factors that can affect reliability:

- **the assessment may not be carried out uniformly**
- **the way that the assessment is explained and introduced can influence the students**
- **subjective or inconsistent marking**
- **students "switching off" and not co-operating**

- **lack of feedback to tutors and students**
- **students' fear of failure**
- **students' previous experience and attitude to 'tests'.**

Careful consideration should be given to ways of minimising these effects. Staff development is crucial in this process.

What are the staff development issues?

Whichever method of screening is used, it is important that all staff have opportunities to reflect on aspects of screening. Staff development can focus on:

- **raising awareness of the need for the early identification of difficulties**
- **the limitations of any screening method that is used in terms of the information that it can give**
- **the interpretation of screening results and how to approach this sensitively with students**
- **exploration of the strategies that are available for supporting students**
- **ways of adapting the course content and delivery methods to assist students' development**
- **defining the role of specialist basic skills staff and how this can be supported by vocational/course staff.**

These issues may be addressed through information and discussion at course meetings or staff meetings.

The organisation and effectiveness of the screening should be evaluated and modifications made in the light of comments received. In this way, the system will develop and increase in its effectiveness.

Devising a course specific assessment

Before embarking on devising a course specific assessment a number of fundamental questions need to be asked:

- **What is the purpose of assessment?**
- **How long will it be and who will mark it?**
- **How will it be followed up and the results fed back to students?**
- **If it involves numeracy, can a calculator be used?**
- **How much written language will be used to set mathematical problems?**
- **Which mathematical terms is it reasonable to expect students to know?**
- **What will the cost be in terms of staff time to devise, administer and mark the assessment as well as the cost of desk top publishing and reproducing it?**

These factors need to be considered:

- There needs to be a collaborative venture between vocational staff and basic skills staff. These may include specialist communication, second language and numeracy tutors. In this way relevant skills and knowledge can be utilised and all tutors will have ownership of the assessment and a stake in ensuring that it is the right tool for the job.

- An analysis of the skills needed at the start of a course should be carried out in a thorough way. It is important to distinguish clearly between the skills needed on entry and the skills that the students are expected to develop during the course. Both sets of data are essential when subsequent judgements are made about the student and advice is given as to the appropriate level of course. This distinction will also aid decisions about the type of support offered to students.

- A common format for auditing the skills required should be used across the vocational areas so that the generic elements of courses can be established.

- Expectations of what information the assessment will provide and how this will be used by the various parties needs to be agreed. If the assessment is being used as an aid to admission, then the information gained should also be available for negotiating the learning goals of the students. Where additional support is needed, the assessment activities might form a useful starting point for devising an individual learning plan. Where a number of students have similar difficulties, an input to the whole group either by a specialist or the course tutor can be built into the planning of the course.

- It is easier to devise objective 'tests' for numeracy than it is for communications. Clear guidelines need to be developed for the assessment of writing skills given that a series of judgements need to be made about the composition of the work, spelling, grammar etc. This will increase the time needed to mark the students' work. Many writing skills can not be marked reliably without considerable specialist time being involved. The testing of students' oral and listening skills is also time consuming and difficult to administer but of vital importance in the vocational education context particularly for ESOL students.

- This kind of analytical approach to assessing the student's level of skills against the demands of the course needs to extend throughout the year so that staff are aware of individual difficulties as they arise.

- Assessments should be piloted for validity with existing students and the results checked against staff perceptions of the students. The tasks should be examined carefully for any gender or cultural bias.

- The assessment should be monitored and evaluated carefully when it is used and its reliability as a useful tool in predicting final outcomes on a course assessed.

A variety of assessment methods can be employed. These include multiple choice questions, cloze passages, free writing, dictation, choosing the correct word, straightforward computation, written mathematical problems, measuring activities, the use of specific mathematical formulae, etc.

An example of a communications assessment developed for Leisure and Recreation course:

Read the passage carefully and answer the questions following:

Section 2

The Dangers of the Western Diet

The Western diet, typified by a hamburger, french fries, a thick milk shake and a slice of cream-topped cheesecake, is one of the potentially dangerous excesses. High in calories, saturated fats, sugar and salt, but low in fibre, it puts its consumers at risk from the two problems of western health, namely obesity and heart and circulatory disease.

The excess energy in the western diet comes from fats, which are undoubtedly implicated in heart disease, and sugar. Sugar is an ingredient of not only obvious foods, such as cheesecake and apple pie, but of processed relishes and ketchups and of factory made hamburgers. In fact, sugar is present in all manner of processed foods, from curry to chicken soup and from baked beans to barbecue sauce. When buying food for home consumption, look at the label (the sugar may be described as glucose, caramel, maltose or fructose).

The problem with sugar is twofold. Firstly, it is a concealed energy source, and eating concealed sugar is a hindrance to those on the verge of serious obesity. Secondly, sugar is the single greatest cause of dental decay. If average sugar consumption in the west was cut from its present 37 kg (81 lb) a year to 20 kg (44 lb), the disease could be significantly reduced.

Using the information from the passage, answer the following questions:

1. What does a typical western meal consist of?(4)

2. The 'western diet' is high in which ingredients?(3)

3. Which dietary element is the western diet low in?(1)

4. Which part of the body is most vulnerable when eating this type of diet?(1)

5. What ingredient is present in most food, although not always obviously?(1)

6. When purchasing food, what would tell you exactly what the food contains?(1)

7. Name three types of sugar(3)

8. In your own words, describe why we need sugar(2)

9. To what extent must we cut down our sugar intake to significantly reduce the risk of heart disease?(2)

Students who have a low score in this exercise would then need to have a further assessment done by a specialist looking at the reading strategies that they were using. Suggestions of how to improve the student's reading could then be incorporated into an Individual Learning Plan.

An example of a Mathematics Assessment developed for Horticulture:

21. What weight of fertiliser should be applied to a plot measuring 120 sq ft if the packet says "apply 2 oz/sq ft"?

22. This year the spring flowers are to be planted in the ratio 3 pansies to 5 tulips. If 60 pansies are to be planted how many tulips will be required?

23. Raspberry canes should be planted 2 ft apart. How many are needed for a row 26 ft long?

Whichever method of screening is used, where students' basic skills are at a level where they will require additional support to complete their chosen course of study, a detailed analysis of the students' difficulties needs to be formulated into an individual learning plan.

3 | *Individual learning plans*

- What needs to be included?
- The Individual Learning Plan
- Involving course tutors in the process

Following up screening with further assessment activities that will provide the information to produce a learning plan that is relevant to each student will be examined in this chapter.

Screening is a useful tool to identify students who need support but it is a crude measure and does not provide a tangible starting point for support work.

Here are some of the worries often expressed by students:

I've read this page twice and I still can't remember a thing.

In lectures I either write everything down the tutor says or I write nothing at all.

I don't know where to start my essay. I'm just not sure of the best way to do it.

I left school ten years ago and I've not done much maths since. I've forgotten how to work out percentages

Because my spelling is bad, I find it difficult to write in the way that I would like. I tend to stick to the words that I know.

Individual learning plans are produced after further assessment aimed at identifying skills gaps and suggesting learning strategies and resources to address these. These are then structured into a plan which defines and prioritises the aims of individual students and sets targets for development.

Further assessment may include:

- **using the information from course specific assessments that have been devised as a basis for discussion with the student**

- **analysing information from an assignment that the student or the course tutor feels highlights difficulties**

- **building up a profile of the student from an informal interview. Attitudes to previous educational experience and the current course of study might be usefully explored at this stage**

- **self assessment by the student of their perceived difficulties and any strategies that they already use to overcome these**

- **relevant assessment tasks such as the Basic Skills Assessment Pack or other graded assessment activities**

- **miscue analysis**

- **spelling error analysis.**

What needs to be included as part of an Individual Learning Plan?

The Individual Learning Plan is the result of negotiation between the student and the support tutor. It is vital that it should link directly to the skills that need to be developed on the student's course. It is desirable that the course tutor should have some kind of input into the plan and be involved in some way in reviewing and updating the plan. If this is not possible, then the plan should relate to the student's perception of the difficulties that they are facing on the course and to other known information about the skills needed to function effectively on the course and complete any given assessment activities. This could come from vocational checklist information and any course profiling done as a result of this (*See Chapter 7*).

Individual Learning Plans can be in a booklet form that is aimed at linking the student's assessment, learning, evaluation and review processes together.

The Learning Plan should contain:

- **the aims of the student and the member of staff responsible for negotiating the learning plan**

- **the student's perceptions of their strengths and weaknesses particularly in relation to their course**

- **the priority areas for development**

- **the skills to be developed, broken down into manageable steps with suggestions of learning strategies that might be useful**

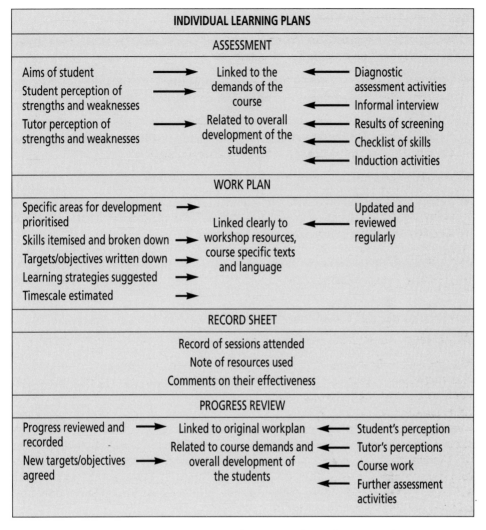

INDIVIDUAL LEARNING PLANS		
ASSESSMENT		
Aims of student $\longrightarrow$ Student perception of strengths and weaknesses $\longrightarrow$ Tutor perception of strengths and weaknesses $\longrightarrow$	Linked to the demands of the course Related to overall development of the students	$\longleftarrow$ Diagnostic assessment activities $\longleftarrow$ Informal interview $\longleftarrow$ Results of screening $\longleftarrow$ Checklist of skills $\longleftarrow$ Induction activities
WORK PLAN		
Specific areas for development prioritised $\longrightarrow$ Skills itemised and broken down $\longrightarrow$ Targets/objectives written down $\longrightarrow$ Learning strategies suggested $\longrightarrow$ Timescale estimated $\longrightarrow$	Linked clearly to workshop resources, course specific texts and language	$\longleftarrow$ Updated and reviewed regularly
RECORD SHEET		
Record of sessions attended Note of resources used Comments on their effectiveness		
PROGRESS REVIEW		
Progress reviewed and recorded $\longrightarrow$ New targets/objectives agreed $\longrightarrow$	Linked to original workplan Related to course demands and overall development of the students	$\longleftarrow$ Student's perception $\longleftarrow$ Tutor's perceptions $\longleftarrow$ Course work $\longleftarrow$ Further assessment activities

- **an estimation of the time needed to complete the agreed activities**

- **some suggestions of resources that might be useful**

- **a way of reviewing and recording progress.**

It is important that the Individual Learning Plan is seen as a working document. It is there to provide a clear structure for the student's learning so that goals can be agreed and realistic targets set. It also needs to be flexible enough to respond to the needs of the student as they change and as other areas of difficulty are encountered on the course.

It is an agreed contract between the member of staff and the student and it outlines the commitment that is needed from the student in terms of time and it also outlines the commitment that the College is prepared to give. It is aimed at promoting independent learning. It provides evidence of learning support activity.

The Individual Learning Plan

Checklists can be developed to help identify the areas that students need to work on. They can be useful for:

- **identifying the extent of the students' difficulties. This is particularly important if additional support funding is to be claimed**

- **helping the students to recognise the extent of the commitment that they will have to make**

- **recording information gained in the assessment process**

- **acting as a useful prompt for the student and helping them to focus on the whole range of communication and numeracy skills that are needed for their particular course.**

Checklists can be devised for all areas of communication and numeracy.

COMMUNICATION SKILLS CHECKLIST		
Student's name:		
Assessor:..		
Date:		
Long Term Aims		
Short Term Aims		
Punctuation	Competent	Needs Revision
Capital letters – sentences		
– proper nouns		
Full stops		
Commas		
Apostrophes – contractions		
– possessions		
Question Marks		

This information then needs to be translated into a workable plan that is easy for the student to follow. It should relate the skill that is being learned to an application that is relevant to the student's course.

WORK PLAN				
Objectives	Agreed No. of hours	Specific Goals/Targets	Resources	Date completed

The student then needs to keep a record of the work that they have done with comments about the resources that they have used and whether these were effective. This record keeping is useful for a variety of reasons:

- **it encourages the student to reflect on and evaluate the learning process and how this has been helped by particular resources**

- **it provides additional information when students come to review their progress and helps with the planning of further goals**

- **it gives both tutors and students a clear idea about the exact stage that the student has reached in the learning plan.**

RECORD SHEET			
Objectives	Task	Recources used	Students' comments

It is this section of the learning plan that it is notoriously difficult to get students to complete! Staff will need to give students a lot of encouragement and plenty of reminders. Helping students to evaluate the resources used can also give them insight into the learning process and their preferred learning styles. It can also help the staff to look at which resources are popular and effective with students.

Without this reflection and evaluation a vital stage in the learning process will be missing and students will not progress towards more self-directed learning.

Progress will need to be reviewed on a regular basis. When this happens is negotiable, but it is helpful to the student if it is after about 40 hours of tuition. Once every half term would be ideal to maintain motivation and ensure that the learning plan is supporting the student's development on their course. Measuring the learning gain of the student against their stated objectives should include discussion about how these new skills have been applied on the student's course and what improvements the student has seen. New areas can then be identified and the learning plan renegotiated.

PROGRESS REVIEW			
Name...			
Date	Goals/Targets	New goals	Signatures of students and tutors
Course/Vocational Tutor's comments:–			

Involving course tutors in the process

Where basic skills tutors are part of course teams or have a liaison role with vocational areas, this can be facilitated more easily. The course tutor should be involved in all stages of the process. The danger is, however, that once the students have been referred for basic skills support then the course tutor feels that the responsibility is no longer theirs. Ensuring that the support is relevant to students and the course, requires examples of course related materials for students to use for extra practice, ideas of the skills that the students will need to complete future assignments etc. You can:

- **send a copy of the work plan sheet to the course tutor and make suggestions of how they could contribute materials and help to reinforce the students' goals**

- **send a copy of the progress sheet either so that the student can discuss this with the tutor or the tutor can add comments in the light of areas that are coming up on the course.**

Sustaining a dialogue in this way encourages tutor involvement and ensures that the vocational dimension is maintained in as relevant a way as possible. It helps both the course tutor and the basic skills tutor to develop their understanding of the student's learning programme and take into account the specific areas that the student is hoping to improve. It gives the course tutor or the personal tutor a more holistic view of the student which can help when students are reviewing their progress within the College for the Record of Achievement. This type of activity then needs to be set into the context of the whole college support system.

4 | *Developing Support*

- Factors influencing the development of support
- Models of support
- How much support do students need?
- Nationally accredited staff training
- Quality Standards in basic skills
- GNVQ core skills and basic skills
- Accreditation of basic skills
- Establishing a cross-college role
- Monitoring and evaluating support
- How can the success of basic skills support be measured?

This chapter will look at the essential ingredients within a basic skills support system. It is clear that if this is to be successful, a number of strategies have to be developed. Relying on workshops alone will not be sufficient. Support needs to be developed at a number of levels.

Devising a structure requires extensive planning to ensure that common practices exist across a college. Where this planning has not been coordinated, pockets of good practice might exist in some vocational areas whereas in others little is done. This lack of cohesion puts some students at a disadvantage and leaves some staff unsupported. Several strategies also need to be developed to account for the students' preferences, cost implications and staff expertise.

There has to be a clear commitment by senior management to the development of support. This is reflected in policies with practical implementation strategies; the monitoring and evaluation of support through Management Information Systems (MIS) and the Quality Assurance process; the timetabling procedure; and inclusion of basic skills issues into the planning of the college.

It is the responsibility of all staff to develop their awareness of basic skills and to take pro-active measures to improve their own skills and knowledge of this area of work. This might include learning new skills, examining their own teaching strategies, course structures and learning materials to ensure that they are supporting students' development. This could mean the inclusion of basic skills staff on course teams to advise on course planning and materials development. There should also be opportunities to enhance development through accredited staff training and in-house staff development opportunities.

Factors influencing the development of support

There are a number of factors that influence how support is developed in colleges:

- the size of the college in terms of the number of students

- the location of college accommodation: whether there are several small satellite sites housing different vocational areas; just a single campus or several main sites spread over a wide geographical area

- the curriculum offer of the college

- the specialist nature of the college eg Agricultural, Building, etc.

- the existing expertise within the college in terms of trained basic skills staff

- the model that the college is adopting for the delivery of GNVQ core skills

- any existing workshop or Resource Based Learning facilities.

Models of Support

There are the three main strands of support:

- **Workshop**

- **On-course Support (Students)**

- **On-course Support (Staff/Sector).**

These strands aim to:

- provide support for individuals that is clearly course related

- work with staff to improve the delivery of courses and presentation of materials

- increase basic skills tutors' knowledge of vocational courses which can then inform workshop practice and on-course support for students

- develop an insight into basic skills practice that enables vocational staff to provide better counselling for students and present a positive image of support

- build partnerships between basic skills and vocational tutors

- devise coherent strategies that meet the needs of different vocational areas.

These three strands of support interrelate and make use of information and expertise gained in one area to develop support in another. Having a number of ways of examining support needs and of delivering an appropriate programme ensures that students can benefit from more than one type of support.

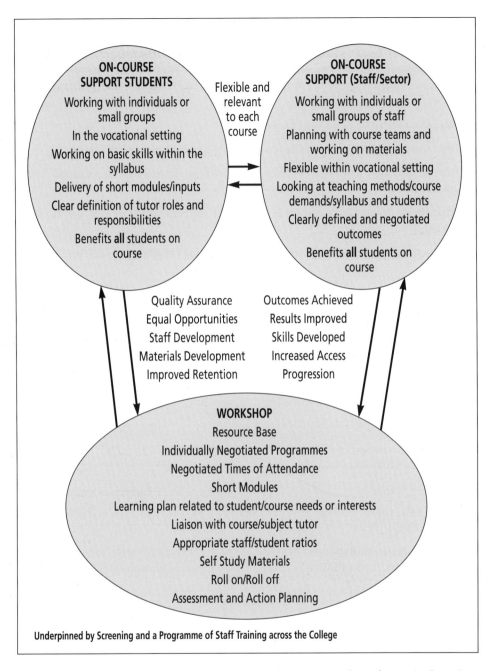

ON-COURSE SUPPORT STUDENTS

Working with individuals or small groups

In the vocational setting

Working on basic skills within the syllabus

Delivery of short modules/inputs

Clear definition of tutor roles and responsibilities

Benefits **all** students on course

Flexible and relevant to each course

ON-COURSE SUPPORT (Staff/Sector)

Working with individuals or small groups of staff

Planning with course teams and working on materials

Flexible within vocational setting

Looking at teaching methods/course demands/syllabus and students

Clearly defined and negotiated outcomes

Benefits **all** students on course

Quality Assurance
Equal Opportunities
Staff Development
Materials Development
Improved Retention

Outcomes Achieved
Results Improved
Skills Developed
Increased Access
Progression

WORKSHOP

Resource Base

Individually Negotiated Programmes

Negotiated Times of Attendance

Short Modules

Learning plan related to student/course needs or interests

Liaison with course/subject tutor

Appropriate staff/student ratios

Self Study Materials

Roll on/Roll off

Assessment and Action Planning

Underpinned by Screening and a Programme of Staff Training across the College

It is important that additional support is seen as integral to the main learning programme, so that support provided relates to the demands and curriculum of the student's course and the goal of the student. Access to workshops has to be seen as part of the course timetable. Any additional staffing within courses should be targeted as far as possible to areas of the course, or particular phases, where basic skills needs are likely to arise. An obvious example is in the preparation of assignments.

How much support do students need?

Students with basic skills at Pre-Foundation or Foundation Level (ALBSU Standards)

Support needs would include:

COMMUNICATIONS	NUMERACY
• Study skills	• Four rules of number
• Note taking/note making	• Fractions
• Spelling strategies	• Decimals
• Reading skills	• Simple percentages
• Reference skills	• Calculator use
• Handwriting	• Estimation
• Sentence structure	• Measurement (metric and imperial)
• Grammar	• Perimeter, areas and volumes
• Punctuation	• Calculations involving units of time
• Paragraphing	• Study skills
• Planning writing	• The language of maths
• Vocabulary development	• Extracting information from tables charts and graphs
• Oral presentation skills	• Calculations involving units of time
• Form filling	

Type of support offered:

- **on-course support by basic skills staff**
- **separate discrete basic skills sessions**
- **timetabled regular tutor support in workshops**
- **reinforcement from course tutor**
- **reinforcement and progress review.**

Support, at this level, would be mainly delivered in the context of the course and could be 'front-loaded' to enable students to concentrate more on basic skills improvement at the beginning of their course.

At this level, the balance of mode of basic skills support could be:

LEVEL	ASSESSMENT/REVIEW	WORKSHOP	ON-COURSE
Pre-FOUNDATION	10 hours	50 hours	225 hours
FOUNDATION	10 hours	75 hours	150 hours

Students with basic skills at Level 1 (ALBSU Standards)

Support needs would include:

COMMUNICATIONS	NUMERACY
• Note taking/note making • Exam techniques • Effective reading eg identifying main points, fact and opinion, intention and meaning • Reference skills • Vocabulary development • Grammar • Spelling strategies • Punctuation • Planning different types of writing • Oral presentation skills • Handwriting	• Study skills • The language of maths • Whole numbers (the 4 rules and problem solving) • Estimation • Using tables, graphs and charts (including conversion) • Measurement (metric and imperial) • Fractions • Decimals • Percentages (simple) • Perimeters, areas and volume • Introduction to simple formulae • Collecting, sorting and presenting data • Averages, range • Calculator use • Ratio • Calculations involving unit of time

Type of support offered:

- **timetabled regular tutor support in workshops**
- **some on-course support from course tutor and basic skills tutor**
- **reinforcement from course tutor**
- **regular assessment and progress review.**

At this level, students would be able to benefit more from a workshop setting although some on-course support would also be needed in particular circumstances.

At this level, the balance of mode of basic skills support could be:

LEVEL	ASSESSMENT/REVIEW	WORKSHOP	ON-COURSE
Level 1	15 hours	100 hours	75 hours

Students with basic skills at Levels 2 & 3 of the ALBSU Standards are likely to be able to cope independently on their course. Although they may have gaps in their basic skills, these may be tackled by the students themselves in workshops, or with support from their tutor.

Support needs might include:

COMMUNICATIONS	NUMERACY
<ul><li>Exam techniques</li><li>Essay planning and writing particularly discursive</li><li>Note taking/note making</li><li>Time management</li><li>Effective reading eg SQ3R</li><li>Spelling strategies</li><li>Punctuation</li><li>Vocabulary development</li><li>Specific aspects of grammar</li></ul>	<ul><li>Study skills</li><li>The language of maths</li><li>Estimating</li><li>Using and constructing tables, charts and graphs</li><li>Measurement</li><li>Conversions</li><li>Problem solving (whole numbers simple formulae)</li><li>Solving equations</li><li>Perimeters, area and volume</li><li>Fractions</li><li>Decimals</li><li>Percentages</li><li>Collecting, organising, interpreting and presenting data</li><li>Averages, range</li><li>Algebra</li><li>Calculator use</li></ul>

Looking at students in this way can be useful so that a realistic view can be formed of all the resources needed for supporting students. It also shows how a variety of strategies will be needed that take account of different methods and material resources. As the student's skills develop the responsibility for support increasingly falls to the course tutor and the student.

Where students have low attainment in basic communication and numeracy skills, considerable input will be needed from specialist tutors on a regular basis to ensure skills development. Course tutors will still have a significant part to play in reinforcing basic skills work and in ensuring that the course planning, delivery and materials take into account the needs of the student group.

Nationally Accredited Staff Training

Staff Development can be facilitated in a number of ways:

- **through partnership teaching**
- **through on-course support**
- **through staff meetings**
- **through in-house short courses on specific topics eg screening**
- **through nationally recognised certificates specific to the teaching of basic skills.**

As a minimum basic skills qualification for specialist basic skills tutors ALBSU recommend the Initial Certificate in Teaching Basic Communications Skills. There are three Initial Certificates:

- **9282 (Literacy)**
- **9283 (Numeracy)**
- **9284 (ESOL).**

They have generic elements to them and more than one of the specialised set of modules can be studied if expertise is to be accredited in more than one area. The courses are accredited by City & Guilds and combine a mixture of taught units, assignments and observed teaching. The structure of the courses and their content is shown opposite.

A new certificate is being piloted which is specifically designed to enable vocational tutors to identify and support students whose basic skills may inhibit their performance on their courses.

This certificate will offer a way of helping course tutors to embed basic skills support within the structure of their courses, in the materials and the delivery. It will not make vocational tutors into basic skills specialists. This kind of training is designed to promote particular outcomes for both staff and students *(see flow chart opposite)*.

City and Guilds Certificate in Teaching Basic Skills

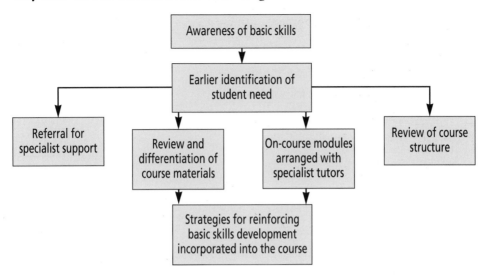

The City & Guilds 9285 'The Certificate in Teaching Basic Skills' is a comprehensive certificate designed for more experienced basic skills staff. It has five units or phases:

Phase A **Identify Learning Needs**

Phase B **Design Learning Programmes**

Phase C **Provide Learning Opportunities**

Phase D **Evaluate Learning**

Phase E **Co-ordinate and Organise**

Phase E is optional as not all basic skills practitioners will have the opportunity to develop in this area.

The 9285 accredits the ALBSU Standards for Basic Skills Teachers. These Standards:

> *"describe the competence of basic skills teachers and provide information on the skills, knowledge and understanding which must be possessed or acquired in order that evidence of competence can be presented."*   The ALBSU Standards for Basic Skills Teachers.

These courses offer a structure for professional development to tutors who are involved with the delivery of basic skills. They offer a way of developing and accrediting the skills of both specialist basic skills tutors and vocational tutors. In this way, support for students can be incorporated into all courses at some level and the expertise of basic skills staff directed towards those students who need considerable help.

Quality Standards in Basic Skills

Every person taking part in a basic skills programme should be entitled to:-

1. A confidential, personal interview before beginning tuition
2. A learning opportunity within easy reach of home
3. At least four hours direct tuition a week
4. An appropriate teacher/student ration in a learning group
5. Respect for gender and cultural identity
6. A negotiated learning plan
7. Regular assessment of progress
8. Access to progression including advice and guidance
9. Access to accreditation
10. Teaching by staff trained to nationally recognised standards
11. Access to suitable learning material
12. Teaching which takes account of the context for learning

AN ALBSU RECOGNISED
QUALITY PROGRAMME

These standards would ensure that a range of suitably located provision was available for students that is accessible and relevant to their needs.

GNVQ Core Skills and Basic Skills

Careful thought needs to be given to any differentiation of these. Are they the same thing or are there differences? How can we make it clear to students and staff what this terminology means? Can definitions help us?

GNVQ Core Skills

There are six core skill areas within the GNVQ framework. The three mandatory units are:

- **Communication**
- **Application of Number**
- **Information Technology.**

The two recommended units which can be included as additional units on GNVQ programme are:

Personal Skills - working with others

Personal Skills - improving own learning and performance.

The sixth unit 'problem solving' has not yet been accredited and NCVQ (National Council for Vocational Qualifications) is carrying out further development work.

Core skills are defined as:

> *"A set of transferable skills considered central to academic, vocational and personal development; emphasis on process/abilities."*
>
> NCC

Basic skills as outlined by ALBSU (*see Chapter one*) have been clearly defined and incorporated into the Basic Skills Standards for Students and Trainees, which can be accredited by Wordpower and Numberpower.

> *"The Standards provide a description of how individuals use communication skills and apply number. At the same time they can provide statements about what is expected of an individual who is using communication and number skills competently. These Standards derive from the functions of communication and number in adult life."*
>
> The ALBSU Standards for Basic Skills Students and Trainees

Although basic skills teaching is concerned solely with communications and numeracy teaching, the delivery methods and individual goal setting also could incorporate elements of other core skills units.

The way that goals are negotiated with students, forming the basis of the individual learning plan that outlines basic skills to be developed and useful strategies and materials for assisting in this, helps students to take responsibility for their learning. Progress can then be recorded against the student's objectives. This is very much in tune with the 'Personal Skills – improving own learning and performance'.

IMPROVING OWN LEARNING AND PERFORMANCE LEVEL 2

Element 2.1: Contribute to the process of identifying strengths and weaknesses and of identifying short-term targets

Performance criteria:

1. the accuracy of own understanding of targets is confirmed with the person(s) setting them

2. information relevant to accurate identification of strengths and weaknesses is provided on request

3. information provided is based on appropriate evidence

4. information relevant to setting appropriate targets is provided on request

Range:

Targets: short -term targets identified by others with a contribution from the individual

Information relevant to target-setting: on own preferences; on progress of work; on features of the working situation

It is useful to think of basic skills and core skills as a continuum with basic skills underpinning those core skills as expressed by the NCVQ performance criteria in Communication and the Application of Number. These examples show how the ALBSU Standards relate to GNVQ competences and help staff and students to identify the basic skills that need to be worked on to achieve an improvement in the student's performance.

NCVQ Performance criteria Communication Level 2	Underpinning knowledge ALBSU Standards Communication
Element 2.2: Prepare written material on routine matters. **Performance criteria:** 1. all necessary information is included and information is accurate 2. documents are legible 3. grammar and punctuation follow standard conventions, and words used routinely are spelled correctly 4. the format used is appropriate to the nature of the material and information is ordered appropriately to maximise audience understanding **Range:** **Subject matters:** routine matters (eg day-to-day organisation and administration; responding to customers' letters). **Format:** pre-set formats (eg record and report cards, memos); outline formats (eg letters, reports, log book entries). **Conventions:** use of full stop, comma, apostrophe, capital letters, sentences and paragraphs. **Audience:** people familiar with the subject matter and in frequent contact with the individual (eg supervisors, colleagues, peers, tutors); people familiar with the subject matter and but not in frequent contact with the individual (eg some customers/clients).	**UNIT 15.1** – *Complete forms* Students/trainees will be expected to know: • purposes of forms • what to expect from different sorts of forms • specialist vocabulary • common abbreviations • drafting techniques • grammatical sentence construction • importance of logical sequencing • use of punctuation • necessary content • where to locate additional sources of information • appropriate context cues can be used to obtain information • skimming and scanning skills • how to summarise information appropriately for purpose • proof reading to make sure instructions have been followed • proof reading for spelling, punctuation and grammar

NCVQ Performance criteria Application of Number Level 1	Underpinning knowledge ALBSU Standards Numeracy
Element 1.2: Represent and tackle problems at core skills level 1	**UNIT 11.3** – *Calculate areas of rectangles and triangles*
Performance criteria:	Students/trainees will be expected to know:
1. techniques appropriate to the task are selected and used by the individual	• area is square units
2. activities required by the techniques are performed to appropriate levels of precision and in the correct sequence	• formulae for areas of rectangles, triangles • units of measure: millimetres, centimetres, metres; inches, feet, yards and their value
3. mathematical terms and mathematical aspects of everyday language are used and interpreted with precision (AT1 3b)	• units of area: square millimetres, square centimetres, square metres; square inches, square feet, square yards and their value
4. use estimation to check calculations (AT2 4c)	
5. calculations and results obtained are correct	• key words/abbreviations, eg square millimetres – mm2, square feet – sq ft, formula, base, perpendicular, height
6. aids are used correctly	• how to write units of area: mm, cm, m, sq ins, sq ft, sq yds
7. conclusions/generalisations/predictions drawn from results are valid	• how to recognise rectangles and triangles in shapes
8. clear justification is given for the interpretation of results	• how to divide up shapes to calculate areas
Range:	• how to multiply lengths
Techniques:	• how to divide lengths
• Solve whole-number problems involving addition and subtraction (AT2 2b).	• how to substitute lengths in formula for area of triangle
• Solve problems involving multiplication and division (AT2 3c).	• how to recognise base and perpendicular height of triangle
• Use fractions, decimals and percentages to describe situations (AT2 4c).	• how to add square units of area
• Use simple formulae expressed in words (AT3 4b).	• how to read calculator displays and symbols: + – x =
• Find perimeters, areas and volumes (AT4 4d).	

Accreditation of Basic Skills

Students who need additional support for basic skills are enrolled on other college courses. Although they need sustained teaching to develop their basic skills, this is not usually part of the students' primary learning goal.

Who might benefit from accreditation?

- A student on a course such as an NVQ course where there is no separate communications or numeracy accreditation as part of that course. Many of the individual Basic Skills Standards can be integrated into the vocational course and accredited alongside the NVQ performance criteria.

- Students who come into the workshop for support and who want to build their skills to a level that enables them to go on to GCSE and who want a bridging accreditation.

- Students whose skills are not yet at a level that enable them to reach the standard of GNVQ Level 1 core skills. Foundation Level Wordpower and Numberpower would enable students to work towards accreditation within a framework that is supporting their communication and numeracy skills development. This could provide a stepping stone onto GNVQ Foundation.

This table shows the relationship of the ALBSU Standards to GNVQ Core Skills.

ALBSU STANDARDS	GNVQ CORE SKILLS
Communication	Communication
Foundation	
Level 1	Level 1 (Foundation)
Level 2	Level 2 (Intermediate)
Level 3	Level 3 (Advanced)
	Level 4
	Level 5

Numeracy	Application of Number
Foundation	
Level 1	Level 1 (Foundation)
Level 2	Level 2 (Intermediate)
	Level 3 (Advanced)
	Level 4
	Level 5

Students who want accreditation for their learning within additional support can renegotiate and have this included as part of their learning goal.

A range of accreditation could be offered including:

- **Wordpower**
- **Numberpower**
- **RSA**
- **Pitman**
- **AEB**
- **Open College Access Network Modules**

The framework of the ALBSU Standards can be used to assess and plan students' work regardless of whether the student attains the full accreditation. Working within this framework has many advantages and can provide:

- Detailed guidance of the underpinning knowledge and expectations of performance at each level. This is useful to check assessment materials against as well as students' work.

- A clear outline of the progression expected between the different levels of the Standards.

- Help for students and tutors in setting realistic goals for development

- Useful criteria for assessing the students skills on entering the programme. Progress can then be measured against these criteria when the student finishes the programme and the learning gain assessed.

- Performance criteria that are context free enabling vocationally related texts and tasks to be used to develop skills.

Evidence from this development can be used later on in the student's career. The skills that are outlined in the ALBSU Standards have been mapped to performance criteria in GNVQ Core Communications and The Application of Number.

Establishing a Cross-College Role

It is important to ensure that colleges organise learning support systems, so that it is easy for all students in need to make use of it. It is essential to have a clear policy outlining students' entitlement to receive support for the assessment and development of their core skills and the underpinning basic skills. Appropriate structures can then be developed to support this, incorporating vocational, communications, IT and numeracy expertise drawn from relevant departments in a college. Basic skills expertise is essential on Core Skills teams.

All of this raises significant issues for management. Existing departmental structures may need to be reviewed so that cross-college learning support teams can be established. These may take responsibility for both additional basic skills support and core skills support. If there is a division of responsibilities, then this needs to be clearly defined and regular liaison and joint planning established.

Establishing a cross-college responsibility can have a number of advantages:

- a manager with overall responsibility for support can develop a strategic view and contribute to the planning process

- resources can be allocated economically

- successful strategies can be disseminated to all members of staff

- a consistency of approach can be developed across the college. This is particularly important for equal opportunities and in monitoring and evaluating the provision

- material resources can be pooled and shared where appropriate

- study modules or self study packages can be developed in response to common areas of difficulty on different courses

- support becomes acknowledged as a mainstream service of the college and can be publicised as such.

Part of this role is to examine the nature of the courses in college with a view to determining not only support for individual students but support for the actual course in the way that it is structured and delivered. This will be examined in more detail in Chapter 7.

Monitoring and Evaluating Support

The support systems that are developed usually require some flexibility and often do not fit exactly into the more rigid structures of traditional courses in terms of student attendance and the use of staff hours. These need to be recorded to:

- **show the usage of workshop time**
- **show evidence of student contact**
- **show evidence of student assessment**
- **provide evidence of students attendance**
- **record student achievement**
- **record reasons for students leaving the provision**
- **show the outcomes of staff involvement on courses.**

This recording can be done manually on:

- **referral sheets**
- **registers**
- **specially designed pro forma**
- **diary sheets**
- **progress review sheets**
- **Individual Learning Plans**
- **Accreditation information.**

Computerised 'swipe card' systems can combine a variety of information about students and enable this information to be utilised from the database in a number of ways to build up a 'profile' of students. Profiles can be built up that analyse a number of factors:

- **reasons for students entering provision**
- **age profile of students**
- **course profile of students**
- **gender profile of students**
- **vocational area breakdown**
- **times of the day when maximum usage occurs**
- **percentage of students achieving their aims**
- **length of stay of students.**

(This can be related to the known level of the students as defined by the *ALBSU Standards*).

In more sophisticated provision, some of this information could be read by an Optical Mark Reader and put onto MIS.

This information is useful in a number of ways and influences:

- **strategies for publicity and marketing**
- **timetabling and staffing**
- **material resource purchase and development.**

How can the success of basic skills support be measured?

Performance indicators in this area will be related to 'value added' measures of student progress. The areas to be recorded and evaluated are shown on the opposite page.

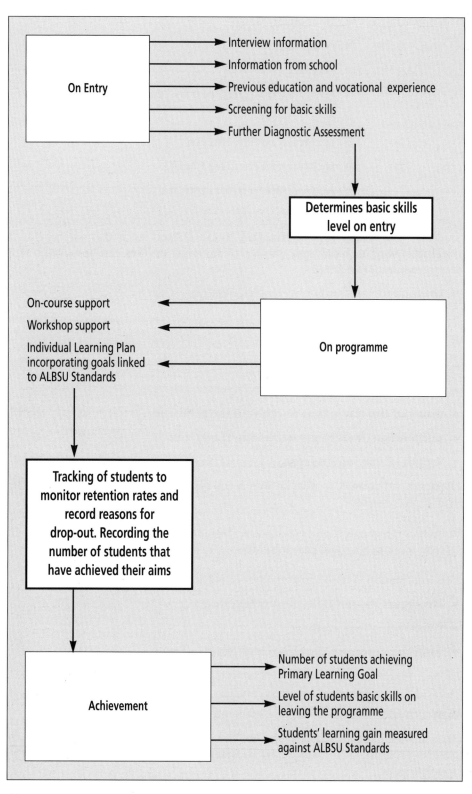

On Entry

→ Interview information
→ Information from school
→ Previous education and vocational experience
→ Screening for basic skills
→ Further Diagnostic Assessment

Determines basic skills level on entry

On programme

← On-course support
← Workshop support
← Individual Learning Plan incorporating goals linked to ALBSU Standards

Tracking of students to monitor retention rates and record reasons for drop-out. Recording the number of students that have achieved their aims

Achievement

→ Number of students achieving Primary Learning Goal
→ Level of students basic skills on leaving the programme
→ Students' learning gain measured against ALBSU Standards

Outcomes of on-course support Staff/Sector and students can be recorded through a 'log' system.

SECTOR SUPPORT LOG

Centre:...

Sector Support Staff:...

Home Sector: ....

Staff:...

Student Support

Initial Contact Date: ....

Purpose of Support: Aims and Objectives..

....

Projected number of hours:...

Planned contact time: Staff.. Students..............................

Total hours spent:...

Work completed on: ....

Outcomes: ....

....

....

Vocational Sector Staff Comment:

REVIEW

Date:

1. Has work been disseminated to other vocational sector staff?.................................

How? (Formal, informal etc.) ....

2. Have any areas of staff development been identified with vocational sector? ....

If so what?..

When delivered?..

3. Have any students been referred to English Workshop?..

Names ....   Dates...

....

....

This clearly shows the use of staff hours and outcomes in terms of materials developed, students referred for support, staff development sessions run, course team meetings attended and their outcomes.

Student and staff satisfaction with the provision also needs to be recorded so that the provision is continually improved in the light of this feedback.

The way that these influences and strategies combine affect the diversity and quality of provision that is offered at a practical level. Practical ways for students to be supported in their basic skills development are examined in the next three chapters.

5 | *Workshop Support*

This chapter will examine the use of workshops to deliver basic skills support for students on college courses. It will try to highlight the issues that need to be considered when developing this style of provision.

Workshop Provision

Workshops that provide additional support for students in communications and numeracy can be run in a variety of ways. They can:

- **combine a flexible facility for primary basic skills students and college students**

- **be integrated into learning resource centres that combine library, IT, Careers and Guidance and tutor support facilities**

- **be incorporated into vocational resource based learning centres**

- **be offered as part of the core skills delivery**

- **be timetabled sessions where students can drop-in for advice and support. These might operate from a classroom rather that a base developed as a workshop and describe the delivery style rather than a physical and material resource.**

Difficulties can arise if these sessions are timetabled at unpopular times of the day ie lunchtimes, early morning or late evening.

The essential features of workshops include:

- **roll-on roll-off provision**

- **flexibility in times of attendance**

- **individually negotiated learning programmes enabling students to work at their own pace and spend extra time on areas of difficulty or special interest**

- a wide range of materials to meet a variety of levels and individual preferences – audio tapes, videos, books, computer software, word processing programmes and worksheets forming the main core of material resources. Better equipped workshops might have interactive video, CD ROM, Cable TV or Camcorders

- a range of accreditation opportunities

- use of the space which allows for one to one assessment, counselling and guidance as well as small group work, audio tape work and oral presentations

- a variety of modes of delivery: students supported on a structured individual learning programme with a low staff/student ratio, specific modules, open learning and self study packages

- staff able to offer support at a variety of levels

- material resources arranged to encourage self access by students

- students monitoring their progress in terms of success

- students receiving help as and when they need it.

What should the workshop be called?

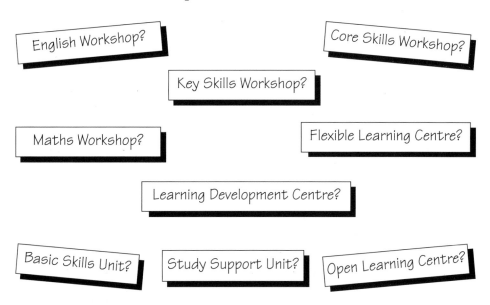

On the face of it this might seem trivial. However, it is not. It is one of the factors that influences the perception of staff and students. Choosing the right name is part of the positive and supportive image you are trying to create.

Does the name explain what goes on in the workshop? It is unlikely that it will be able to convey much in the way of detailed information. What students (and staff) really want to know is:

- **Who is it for?**
- **How can it help me?**
- **Who do I see, if I want to go?**
- **Will it just be like another class?**

These kinds of questions need to be clarified in publicity about the workshop. Explaining the approaches that are used, how they can relate to the student's vocational course and when the workshop is available are vital if the students are to make use of the facility.

Where should the Workshop be located?

This can mean the difference between success and failure. If the workshop is hidden away in an inaccessible part of the building or at a distance from the main site, then this will prevent many students from attending. Ideally it should be part of or attached to a main area of activity in the College. The workshop should also be:

- **Clearly signed**
- **Inviting – with pleasant furnishings and decoration**
- **Arranged so that the layout and furniture is different from that used in a traditional classroom**
- **Easily accessible for all students including those with disabilities.**

This all contributes to the idea that a more flexible way of working happens in the workshop. It may help some students to overcome their fears that starting to work on English and maths again will reinforce the feelings of failure that some of them experienced in the past.

What is the role of the Manager?

The Manager will have an overview of the activity in the workshop and develop the provision so that it is responsive to the needs of the students. They will evaluate the statistical information to ensure effective workshop use and student satisfaction. Systems will need to be developed for monitoring and recording that extend beyond those used for more traditional courses, which recruit at specific times of the year and follow a set pattern of attendance.

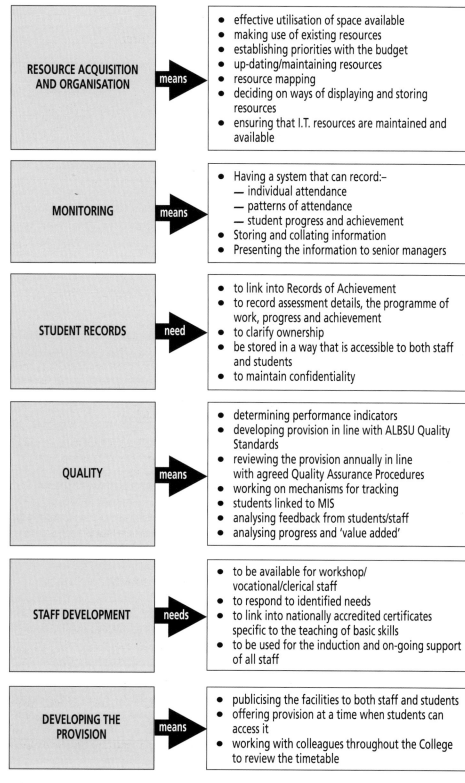

| **RESOURCE ACQUISITION AND ORGANISATION** | means | • effective utilisation of space available
• making use of existing resources
• establishing priorities with the budget
• up-dating/maintaining resources
• resource mapping
• deciding on ways of displaying and storing resources
• ensuring that I.T. resources are maintained and available |

| **MONITORING** | means | • Having a system that can record:–
  — individual attendance
  — patterns of attendance
  — student progress and achievement
• Storing and collating information
• Presenting the information to senior managers |

| **STUDENT RECORDS** | need | • to link into Records of Achievement
• to record assessment details, the programme of work, progress and achievement
• to clarify ownership
• be stored in a way that is accessible to both staff and students
• to maintain confidentiality |

| **QUALITY** | means | • determining performance indicators
• developing provision in line with ALBSU Quality Standards
• reviewing the provision annually in line with agreed Quality Assurance Procedures
• working on mechanisms for tracking
• students linked to MIS
• analysing feedback from students/staff
• analysing progress and 'value added' |

| **STAFF DEVELOPMENT** | needs | • to be available for workshop/vocational/clerical staff
• to respond to identified needs
• to link into nationally accredited certificates specific to the teaching of basic skills
• to be used for the induction and on-going support of all staff |

| **DEVELOPING THE PROVISION** | means | • publicising the facilities to both staff and students
• offering provision at a time when students can access it
• working with colleagues throughout the College to review the timetable |

What is the role of the workshop lecturer?

This will be different from the traditional role of the lecturer.

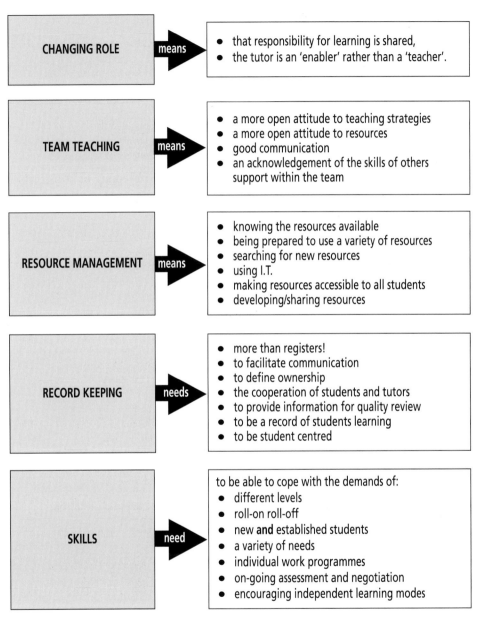

CHANGING ROLE means	• that responsibility for learning is shared, • the tutor is an 'enabler' rather than a 'teacher'.
TEAM TEACHING means	• a more open attitude to teaching strategies • a more open attitude to resources • good communication • an acknowledgement of the skills of others support within the team
RESOURCE MANAGEMENT means	• knowing the resources available • being prepared to use a variety of resources • searching for new resources • using I.T. • making resources accessible to all students • developing/sharing resources
RECORD KEEPING needs	• more than registers! • to facilitate communication • to define ownership • the cooperation of students and tutors • to provide information for quality review • to be a record of students learning • to be student centred
SKILLS need	to be able to cope with the demands of: • different levels • roll-on roll-off • new **and** established students • a variety of needs • individual work programmes • on-going assessment and negotiation • encouraging independent learning modes

In order to facilitate good workshop practice staff should be:

- **able to identify students' needs in terms of strengths and weaknesses through negotiation and initial on-going assessment**
- **able to match students' needs to a variety of learning strategies which suit the individual or group concerned**

- able to match students' needs to appropriate resources (which means being familiar with a wide range of resources so as not to restrict choice) or devising materials to meet those needs

- able to guide the student towards independent modes of learning

- able to play their part in the management and running of the workshop including monitoring and review procedures to ensure quality provision

- flexible in their approach to ensure a wide variety of needs are met in any workshop session

- caring and sensitive to individuals and their barriers to learning and aware of referral possibilities for counselling and guidance

- willing to liaise with course tutors and other providers to maximise learning support opportunities for students.

What about the student?

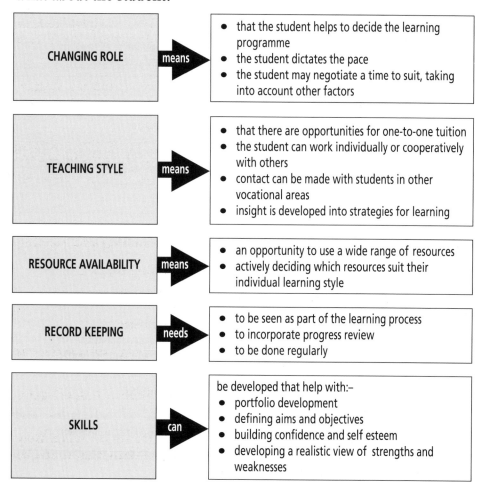

CHANGING ROLE *means*
- that the student helps to decide the learning programme
- the student dictates the pace
- the student may negotiate a time to suit, taking into account other factors

TEACHING STYLE *means*
- that there are opportunities for one-to-one tuition
- the student can work individually or cooperatively with others
- contact can be made with students in other vocational areas
- insight is developed into strategies for learning

RESOURCE AVAILABILITY *means*
- an opportunity to use a wide range of resources
- actively deciding which resources suit their individual learning style

RECORD KEEPING *needs*
- to be seen as part of the learning process
- to incorporate progress review
- to be done regularly

SKILLS *can* be developed that help with:–
- portfolio development
- defining aims and objectives
- building confidence and self esteem
- developing a realistic view of strengths and weaknesses

The student will be expected to take a much more active role in the development of their learning in a workshop.

The benefits to students of this type of approach can be enormous. Where students exercise greater control and choice over their learning means that they are acquiring learning habits that will help them to progress both in a college and an employment context.

Most students will need to learn how to make the most of the opportunities that workshops have to offer. For some this will be very difficult particularly if their level of basic skills is poor or they lack confidence.

The ethos of the workshop needs to be reflected in the way that it is organised and the documentation that is used. The range of abilities of students and the difficulties that they need to address means that some will require frequent guidance and support from the tutor in order to benefit whereas others will function in the workshop with the minimum of tutor input.

The role of initial counselling, guidance and assessment that leads to a well structured learning plan is absolutely critical to the process of helping students to acquire insight into their own learning strategies and so that they can then use these to further develop their basic skills.

There are some questions that we should ask relating to students learning effectively in a workshop setting.

How do we prepare students for independent learning?

We need to have:

- **Clear expectations of the workshop system of teaching and learning**

- **Well structured, 'user friendly' Individual Learning Plans**

- **Frequent opportunities for progress review**

- **Well organised, clearly labelled, accessible resources**

- **Opportunities for students to develop the language of assessment and review**

- **Effective recording mechanisms to facilitate independent, negotiated learning**

- **Techniques for building the students' confidence to ask when they need help and to move about the workshop when they need to access new resources.**

How can we help students determine their needs?

Workshop staff can:

- **Liaise with course tutors to build up a picture of the course content, assessment methods, etc.**
- **Provide self assessment checklists to help students to focus on the specific skill areas that relate to their course**
- **Ensure that assessment activities reflect the level of language and numeracy needed on the course**
- **Help students to reflect on their previous educational and life experience and relate this to their current course.**

Although the emphasis is on students following their individual routes to meet their specific goals, students can support each other in a workshop environment. Ways of encouraging group interaction can also be considered by offering special sessions or modules on specific areas such as spelling strategies, note-taking or exam techniques. For students who need to develop their oral skills, the support of a group is essential.

Basic skills support in a workshop should offer more than just a 'first aid post' for students who are struggling with their assignments. This may be the priority on the first visit but the underlying difficulties that a student is having will need to be addressed, so that skills are developed in a way that will enable the students to apply these to the next assignment task with less staff support.

How are students referred for support?

Students can be referred for basic skills support in a variety of ways:

- **as a result of screening**
- **on the strength of previous educational information about the student**
- **in response to a student's anxieties about their perceived weaknesses**
- **when difficulties become apparent after the first assignment**
- **later in the course when the student finds difficulty with particular aspects of the course.**

It is clear that the importance of the screening and its speedy completion is vital here if the support is to be negotiated at the start of the programme and included in the student's overall Learning Plan. Where screening is done before the course starts, the referral interviews can begin immediately in the induction phase or even have been done before the start of the course.

58

Basic skills support staff need to be able to respond quickly and flexibly to this initial demand.

Preparing the students to start

In a workshop where a number of students will be supported at the same time, there needs to be a preparation phase. If students arrive at their first session without any preliminary procedure, the member of support staff is unlikely to be able to offer the time to establish clear aims, relevant background information and start to develop a learning plan. For students with significant basic skills difficulties this can be quite a time consuming process. Once the starting points have been established, assessment and further planning can be an on-going process with the basic skills lecturer.

In a large workshop organisation, this initial procedure may take place between the student and the coordinator who has responsibility for timetabling and monitoring the provision. The information gained and negotiated learning plan is then be passed on to the workshop staff.

In a smaller organisation the interviewing and tutoring of the student might be done by the same person.

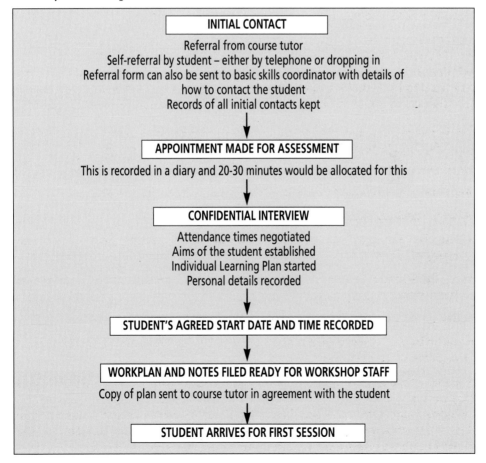

INITIAL CONTACT
Referral from course tutor
Self-referral by student – either by telephone or dropping in
Referral form can also be sent to basic skills coordinator with details of
how to contact the student
Records of all initial contacts kept

↓

APPOINTMENT MADE FOR ASSESSMENT
This is recorded in a diary and 20-30 minutes would be allocated for this

↓

CONFIDENTIAL INTERVIEW
Attendance times negotiated
Aims of the student established
Individual Learning Plan started
Personal details recorded

↓

STUDENT'S AGREED START DATE AND TIME RECORDED

↓

WORKPLAN AND NOTES FILED READY FOR WORKSHOP STAFF
Copy of plan sent to course tutor in agreement with the student

↓

STUDENT ARRIVES FOR FIRST SESSION

Once the student has started on their plan and is familiar with the layout of the workshop, there is no reason why they should not 'drop-in' at other times to use the workshop. They would not be guaranteed staff attention in this situation as the individual lecturer may be involved with another group of students.

Timetabling support for individuals enables the workshop coordinator to maintain a workable staff/student ratio so that students are assured of the level of attention that they need.

As a guide, in the Quality Standards for Basic Skills, ALBSU recommends:

Students' Level of Basic Skills (as defined by the ALBSU Standards)	Staff/student Ratio (Staff means one paid member of staff)
Foundation	6 – 8 students
Level 1	8 – 10 students
Levels 2 and 3	10 – 12 students

Recording all contacts and interviews is essential for:

- **monitoring the use of staff time**

- **evaluating the effectiveness of the procedures**

- **providing end of year figures and evidence of support activity**

- **recording the outcomes of the activity.**

An interview register is useful for this (*see page 62*)

Starting Basic Skills Support

Once this preliminary phase is complete, the student is ready to start to attend on the agreed basis.

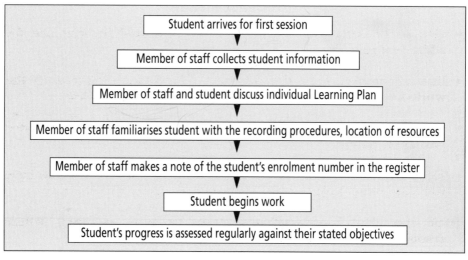

Student arrives for first session

Member of staff collects student information

Member of staff and student discuss individual Learning Plan

Member of staff familiarises student with the recording procedures, location of resources

Member of staff makes a note of the student's enrolment number in the register

Student begins work

Student's progress is assessed regularly against their stated objectives

Organising resources

As well as the individualised approaches already identified through the use of Individual Learning Plans, workshop delivery relies on having a choice of different material resources to cater for a variety of levels of ability in different vocational areas.

These will include:

- **Books**

- **Videos**

- **Audio Tapes**

- **Worksheets**

- **Open Learning packs**

- **A range of computer software.**

These need to be linked in a coherent way to allow students the maximum amount of self access. This is 'resource mapping' or 'routeing'. The organisation of resources should aim to:

- **create a 'user friendly' system that is accessible to all students and staff**

- **clearly define the knowledge that students need to have in each skill area and show the steps needed to achieve this. These ideas can be introduced to students on an initial sheet**

- **identify the resources that will enable the students to acquire that knowledge and learn the skill**

- **give suggestions of further resources that students can use for additional practice**

- **link all resources to the different accreditation offered in the workshop, thus giving them a level**

- **free the staff to spend more time with those students who need particular help**

- **integrate all resources into the system so that students would have the maximum choice within a given area**

- **aid the identification of any 'resource gaps' or areas where resources need updating or extending.**

INTERVIEW REGISTER

Week beginning ---------------

Name	F/T or P/T	Attended	Type of Assessment		Outcome			Assessed by
			Initial	Progress and Guidance	Placed	Referred	Other	
TOTALS								

A resource map could look like this:

7. APOSTROPHE – Possession

What you need to understand:

- You need to understand that an apostrophe is used to show that something is owned by someone or something.

What you need to be able to do:

- You need to be able to apply the rules when using an apostrophe to show possession.
- You need to be able to decide on the correct position of the apostrophe.

First do this:

level		where it is
2	Runcorn Punctuation Pack, Module 2, Apostrophe	Open shelf
3	Worksheets – The Apostrophe's Uses and The Apostrophe	Box 3p Open shelf
	A New English Course (R Jones), p91	Shelf 6

Then do this:

level		where it is
2	Worksheets – Apostrophe No 2 and No 3	Box 3p Open shelf
3	Checkbook Punctuation, p22	Shelf 2

Need more practice? Then do this:

level		where it is
2	Improve English Skills, chapter 24	Shelf 2
3	Assignments in Punctuation, p37	Shelf 2

HELP!

If at any time you need help, ask your tutor

Similar maps would exist for the different literacy and numeracy skills to be developed. Where workshops are well established with a variety of resources in place, this is a considerable task. Where workshops are just being developed, this kind of system can be incorporated from the beginning and extended as the resources grow.

These underpinning basic skills are generic and apply to all vocational areas. However, as well as these general resource maps, additions can be made that are relevant to particular vocational areas. It is also essential to help the students to identify the contexts within which they will be able to use or practise the skills that they are learning.

Using I.T.

Many students use computers to help them to develop their basic skills. Some students will learn a computer skill alongside the basic skills that they are working on thus building up their competence in both areas. For students who have basic computer knowledge, using computers can have several advantages:

- **Much of the tedium can be taken out of writing tasks that require a number of drafts**

- **Work can be stored easily**

- **It can give the work 'status' in the student's eyes**

- **Content free programmes can allow students to work on their own texts or vocationally related texts**

- **Texts can be used that cater for a variety of levels**

- **Many programmes include instant self checking mechanisms**

- **Pairs or small groups of students can collaborate on tasks**

- **Students can work independently for reasonably long periods**

- **Computer time in the workshop can be booked by a whole range of students increasing the use of the facilities**

- **The chart function of spreadsheets and databases can be used to present material in a graphical form**

- **Computer technology eg scanners, storing resources on disk and CD ROM can reduce the need for vast quantities of worksheets and books. It can bring a range of reference and vocational material into the workshop**

As prices decrease and new refinements become available, the use of computer technology will increase and become integral to basic skills support provision. In particular, the development of multi-media authoring systems in some colleges has opened the way to high quality programmes for language and literacy support that use video, audio, graphics and text. Integrated Learning Systems that address basic skills needs are also coming on to the market, and should be considered for use in workshop support.

Barriers to Students using the Workshop for Support

For students to progress in any learning situation they have to want to succeed. Responsibility for student success lies not only with the student but with course tutors and the institution itself. If the ethos of the college is geared towards meeting the needs of individuals then this should be reflected in the college system and the attitudes and skills of staff.

These are some of the barriers that can prevent students from using a workshop and some suggestions of how to overcome them.

STUDENTS	
Barriers	**Possible Solutions**
Lack of information about support available	• Information about support included in College Prospectus, Student Handbook, Staff Handbook. • Visit to workshop included in induction tour.
'Remedial' image of support	• Location of support workshop alongside other mainstream student support activities. • Approach of the College in offering programmes to meet individual's needs.
'English' the last thing they want to do	• Information about all the skills that students will need or be expected to develop whilst on the course – not just the vocational skills. • Clearly relating the skills that the student is developing to those needed on their course.
Memories of school still vivid	• Explanation of the different approaches used – individual learning programmes, working at their own pace, etc.

STAFF	
Barriers	**Possible Solutions**
Unsure of basic skills needs *No guidelines for identifying students with basic skills needs* *Unsure of how to approach students*	A programme of staff development to include:- • Awareness raising about basic skills needs • Screening – its uses and limitations and how to interpret the results • Techniques in counselling and guidance.
Not seen as their role/ responsibility	• An agreed system within the College that clearly defines the role of the course tutor/personal tutor/basic skills staff in the referral and subsequent support and progress review of students.
Lack of knowledge about support available	• Information about support included in Staff Handbook, explained at staff induction, presented by basic skills staff at course team meetings, Faculty meetings, in College newsletters, on posters and handouts.
Not seen as a priority for course/students	• Discussion and evidence about retention and achievement rates and how this will affect courses in the future.
INSTITUTION	
Barriers	**Possible Solutions**
Not high on the list of priorities *Status/profile of the work*	• Presentation to senior managers about evidence of need within the College and strategies for improving retention and achievement rates of students.
Distance to workshop for students not on the main site *Lack of space on the timetable*	• Ensuring that the interests of basic skills support are represented when new developments are being planned, eg resourced based learning centres, new timetabling arrangements.
Not part of course planning *Lack of time for liaison* *Not part of college policy*	• A clear policy of entitlement to support that includes strategies for implementation across the whole college. Inclusion of basic skills support within the college's quality assurance procedures.

Workshop organisation and delivery is a rapidly expanding area in many colleges. There are implications for staff and, as a way of working, workshop teaching will place different demands on them. The roll on – roll off nature of workshops means that demand may vary throughout the year which will require some flexibility in how staff hours are used. The smaller the provision, the more difficult this may become.

The staffing issues that need to be considered are:

- **flexibility offered through an appropriate percentage of core and periphery staff allocated to the workshop**
- **clerical and technician assistance**
- **multi-skilled staff.**

There also needs to be a commitment to supporting staff in this environment through:

- **regular staff meetings**
- **in-house staff development sessions**
- **nationally accredited training specific to the teaching of basic skills**
- **a staff handbook**
- **a mentor system for staff who are new to workshop teaching**
- **a designated coordinator.**

Well organised workshops with relevant resources and staff trained and committed to this way of working can provide excellent support for many students. For students who lack motivation or who are part of a large group of students with similar levels of difficulty needing a significant amount of help, on-course support is another strategy that can be developed.

6 | *On-Course Support (Students)*

- When is this form of support appropriate?
- How are the group/individuals identified?
- What are the roles of the tutors involved?
- Additional Basic Skills Support at key points in a course

In this chapter, the use of partnership teaching will be discussed. This is where basic skills staff work alongside the vocational lecturer to develop the language, literacy and numeracy skills of students in the context of the vocational course.

When is this form of support appropriate?

- **When a significant proportion of students in a group have basic skills levels that are below the level expected on the course. This is particularly important when these students are part of a large class group.**

- **At key points in the course where specific basic skills input would be useful.**

- **When an individual student has been identified as needing one to one support to develop their language skills.**

- **When a small number of students require language support in a group.**

How are the groups/individual students identified?

Students who need on-course support can be identified in a number of ways:

- **by information from the screening**

- **by information contained in previous school records**

- **from discussions with vocational, communications or maths tutors**

- **from information obtained in interviews prior to enrolment on the course.**

What are the roles of the staff involved?

Although the roles of the staff involved will be different, the status of their contribution to the course should be equal.

The Basic Skills Staff role is:-

- **to identify students' basic skills difficulties**

- to help students to recognise their basic skills difficulties and negotiate ways of overcoming these

- to bring the expertise and resources of the basic skills workshop into the class and adapt these to make them vocationally relevant

- to devise strategies to meet individual needs

- to help the partner lecturer to meet the curriculum objectives

- to work closely with the partner lecturer to devise suitable schemes of work and to help to review the scheme throughout the year.

The Partner Lecturer's role is:

- to improve students' communication and numeracy skills both generally and vocationally

- to devise a scheme of work that meets all the course requirements

- to meet the individual needs of the students

- to liaise with the support staff and establish good working patterns that respond to the needs of the group.

Many staff are not used to working alongside another lecturer or being observed whilst teaching. This needs to be handled with sensitivity.

Once the initial rapport has been established, vocational staff can begin to see the benefits of sharing some of the assessment of students and planning of work. Where large numbers of students in a group are having difficulty with a particular topic, the work of the basic skills staff can enhance and support their own teaching.

Various working patterns have been tried. These can be used for partnership teaching that would run throughout the year and also for support at specific points in the course:

- the basic skills staff work to identify the specific needs of students in the group and provide materials and tutorial help to meet these needs

- the class is split in two and each member of staff takes total responsibility for their half for a given period. This works better when the partner tutor is a communications or maths specialist

- small groups of students are withdrawn to work on certain topics. The teaching input is shared by the course tutor giving specific vocational input and supplemented by relevant basic skills input from the support staff.

Working in this way involves planning and liaison at all stages of the course:

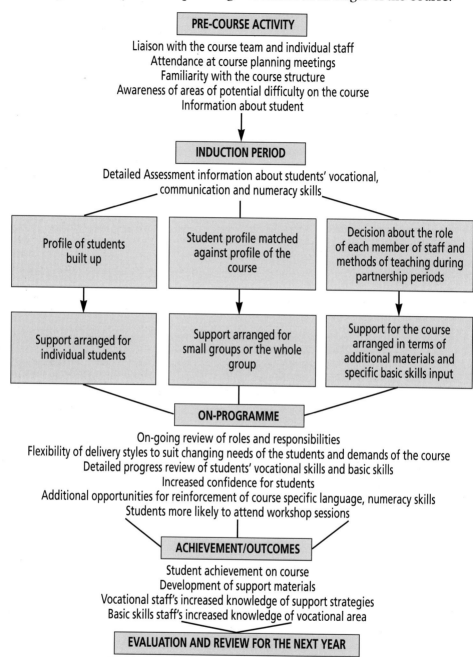

PRE-COURSE ACTIVITY

Liaison with the course team and individual staff
Attendance at course planning meetings
Familiarity with the course structure
Awareness of areas of potential difficulty on the course
Information about student

INDUCTION PERIOD

Detailed Assessment information about students' vocational,
communication and numeracy skills

| Profile of students built up | Student profile matched against profile of the course | Decision about the role of each member of staff and methods of teaching during partnership periods |

| Support arranged for individual students | Support arranged for small groups or the whole group | Support for the course arranged in terms of additional materials and specific basic skills input |

ON-PROGRAMME

On-going review of roles and responsibilities
Flexibility of delivery styles to suit changing needs of the students and demands of the course
Detailed progress review of students' vocational skills and basic skills
Increased confidence for students
Additional opportunities for reinforcement of course specific language, numeracy skills
Students more likely to attend workshop sessions

ACHIEVEMENT/OUTCOMES

Student achievement on course
Development of support materials
Vocational staff's increased knowledge of support strategies
Basic skills staff's increased knowledge of vocational area

EVALUATION AND REVIEW FOR THE NEXT YEAR

Additional Basic Skills Support at key points in a course

Alternatively there may be key times within a course programme when it is highly beneficial to offer additional basic skills support to students. This may be for individual courses or a number of vocationally related courses.

Induction	On-programme
• note-taking skills • time management skills • mathematical concepts or formulae needed to start the course • research skills	• planning and drafting writing • research skills • course specific language • mathematical concepts and formulae • report writing • oral presentation skills • revision skills • exam or test terminology • exam technique

Example One

BTec Media Studies Year One students were struggling with taking notes during lectures at the beginning of the course. The basic skills member of staff developed a subject specific pack on note-taking and planned to deliver it to small groups of students in short sessions that were additional to the course work.

An improvement in the students' skills was noted in the before and after tasks. The pack was available for use with new students the following year.

MISSING OUT UNNECESSARY WORDS

Only words essential to the meaning need to be left in your notes.

e.g. Actors need to wear make-up to stop the glare from the very bright stage lights making their faces look unnaturally pale.

This could be written as:
Make-up – stop glare from v. bright lights making faces pale.

NB. Dashes are very important
Use dashes to separate ideas.

ACTIVITY

Make notes of these sentences leaving out unnecessary words.

1. Make-up is also useful to help actors disguise themselves or to make them look more like the character they are playing.

2. The make-up artist for the theatre generally takes his or her assignments from the stage director who, in the main, controls all aspects of production.

3. Usually the make-up artist does only a specific character or personality backstage as most of the minor players are expected to do their own make-up for each performance.

4. Make-up is more likely to be done in the dressing rooms of the theatre since no specific room is set up as a make-up room.

5. Actors need a large mirror, preferably with light bulbs around the outside, so that they can see their faces clearly while they are putting their make-up on.

Example Two

Motor Vehicle students on City & Guilds 383 found the Industrial Studies Module presented some difficulties and the pass rate was poor. This module was unlike any other on the course and for YT Trainees there was no time on the course for additional communications input. The vocational lecturers felt more comfortable with supporting the development of numeracy skills. The students were expected to research information and structure a piece of writing around a specific topic. The skills needed were:

- **research skills**
- **planning and drafting**
- **legible handwriting**
- **sentence structure and spelling to a reasonable level**
- **structuring the main ideas into a logical order**
- **summarising the main ideas at the end**
- **identifying and interpreting information from:**
  books, leaflets, observation, oral communication – face to face and on the telephone
- **writing letters to request information**
- **reorganising and rephrasing information into their own words.**

TASK NO. 383/22 CITY & GUILDS

ASSIGNMENT TITLES

Task No.

383/22/1 Write about the organisational structure of a typical garage organisation or transport repair workshop, naming the main departments and outlining the roles of the staff employed.

383/22/2 Write about the main services provided by the sales and servicing side of the industry describing distribution channels along which vehicles and accessories pass from manufacturer to user.

383/22/3 Write about the roles of negotiating bodies, employers' organisations and unions within the Vehicle Repair and Retail Industry giving examples of the work undertaken by such organisations.

383/22/4 Write about the importance of building and maintaining good customer relations in the Vehicle Repair and Retail Industry, describing the legal requirement to trade fairly.

383/22/5 Write about the typical career patterns for a person joining the Vehicle Repair and Retail Industry after leaving school describing any opportunities for promotion.

Read through the 5 titles. Ask yourself these questions:–

Which am I really interested in?

Which do I know most about?

Where will I find information from?

Which would I like to find out about?

How can I use my personal experience?

REMEMBER:– If you are not sure about the meaning of a questions –

ASK YOUR TUTOR

The basic skills member of staff structured a pack to support the development of the project and then gave a short input on planning the writing. The vocational lecturer worked on looking at the meaning of the assignment titles and research methods. On three further designated lessons, the basic skills member of staff worked with the vocational lecturer, both giving help on an individual basis to assist the students in developing their projects.

Other sections in the pack also included:

- **planning your assignment**
- **finding information**
- **adding illustrations**
- **writing the assignment – content**
- **writing the assignment – presentation**
- **checking your assignment.**

Help focused on problem areas of the course or at the beginning of the course can pay dividends - improving students' success, developing students' skills and forming links with basic skills support provision that may give students the confidence to use the workshop on other occasions during their course. This is extremely important for those students who are reluctant to use workshop facilities. There are also ways of building support for basic skills development into the structure of courses by working with staff. This benefits all students on a course.

7 | *On-Course Support (Staff/Sector)*

- What are the aims of on-course support (staff/sector)?
- How can this be done?
- Extending the support network
- Analysing the basic skills of courses
- Maximising the effectiveness of teaching methods
- Maximising the effectiveness of resources used
- Developing vocationally relevant resources
- How can skills be developed using a variety of material resources?
- Skills mapping tasks
- Building a partnership between vocational lecturers and basic skills lecturers
- Informing workshop staff

This chapter will examine the need for support to extend beyond that given to individuals or groups of students in a workshop or class setting.

There is ample evidence to support the view that many students struggle on courses with literacy and numeracy skills. This can have a cumulative effect and mean that students fall further and further behind as their motivation decreases.

To concentrate resources solely on workshops will not facilitate the fundamental change that is needed. Students at Foundation Level and Level 1 (ALBSU Standards) will benefit from language development work and numeracy within their vocational area, on vocationally relevant tasks. Support delivered in this way helps to overcome the barriers that students may face in terms of peer group pressure, stigma and previous educational experience.

In developing the three strands of support (detailed in Chapter 4) it is hoped that a larger proportion of students, who are not gaining the maximum benefit from their course, will access the support that they need so that they stay on the course and complete the work successfully.

The three strands of support interrelate and some students – hopefully those who most need it – will benefit from all three strands. This is particularly important for those students who need more support than just time in the workshop which may only be for two or three hours per week. Good motivation heightens the level of functioning in basic skills. Students tend to be more motivated if they are working in their chosen vocational area and can see the relevance of basic skills. The course tutors' role is vitally important in this, particularly where students may encounter difficulties with the course presentation and level of tasks that they are given.

What are the aims of on-course support (Staff/Sector)?

• To extend the support network for students with basic skills difficulties	• To maximise the effectiveness of resources used
• To analyse the basic skills content of courses	• To build partnerships between vocational lecturers and basic skills workshop lecturers
• To maximise the effectiveness of teaching methods	• To inform workshop staff

How can this be done?

Extending the support network

This can be done by:

- contacting key people eg. Faculty Directors, Heads of Schools, Course Coordinators, Programme Managers. These people will have an overview of a course or groups of courses that could benefit from additional support

- building relationships with vocational lecturers. This may be formally through involvement with course planning or staff development, or it may be informally through liaison about individual students, contact in the staff room etc.

- raising awareness of the needs of students with basic skills difficulties and how staff cope with this at present

- looking at how this can be part of a staff development programme within the vocational area.

Analysing the basic skills content of courses

Basic skills are implicit within courses and often tutors expect that students will arrive on the course equipped with these skills so that they need not be taught as part of the course. Many students choose courses in vocational areas where they perceive they will no longer need to develop or even use, to any great extent, English and maths. They have often felt unsuccessful in these areas.

When on a course, basic skills are needed in these three areas:

- *the course content* - eg for a motor vehicle student reading car manuals, following written instructions, listening to and observing practical demonstrations, understanding diagrams, understanding angles;

- *the assessment* – which could require project work, oral explanations, answering multiple choice questions, giving written explanations;

- *the teaching and learning methods* – used on a course might require note-taking or note-making skills, research skills, revision for exams or tests.

Auditing courses is the beginning of looking at a detailed profile of a course. Basic skills and vocational staff should work together to fill out a comprehensive checklist that looks at the course content, assessment requirements and delivery methods. This can provide information that helps the basic skills staff to understand the course and the vocational lecturer to be aware of all the basic skills that students are expected to have on the course.

The extracts below show some examples of the types of questions that could be used as a starting point to build up a profile of a course.

VOCATIONAL COURSE CHECKLIST

General Course Information

Member of staff   Name .... Role ....

Hours working on course ....

Different elements of course:–

	yes	no
modules	☐	☐
taught	☐	☐
practical	☐	☐
open learning	☐	☐
work placement	☐	☐
communication input	☐	☐
numeracy input	☐	☐
I.T. input	☐	☐
other		

How is the course made up and what is your input:......................................

....

Teaching Styles

a. Which teaching styles are used on the course?

Do they include:

	yes	no
lectures	☐	☐
notes	☐	☐
OHP	☐	☐
handouts	☐	☐
demonstrations	☐	☐
dictation	☐	☐
discussion	☐	☐
worksheets	☐	☐
packages	☐	☐
videos	☐	☐
other		

Any comments...

....

b. Are technical terms used on the course?

	yes	no
specialist words	☐	☐
academic language	☐	☐

(give examples) ....

Any comments ....

....

Assessment

How is the course assessed?

Does the assessment include:-

	yes	no
exams (interim or final)	☐	☐
continuous assessment	☐	☐
assignments or project work	☐	☐
practical	☐	☐
oral presentation	☐	☐
placement component	☐	☐
other		

Any comments..

....

Student Requirements

a. Practical Skills

	yes	no
(i) Do students have to translate verbal or written instructions to action?	☐	☐

Any comments ....

....

b. Personal skills

	yes	no
(i) Do students deal with the public or have to communicate with others?	☐	☐

Any comments ....

....

(ii) Do students need to be aware of:-

	yes	no
formal and informal communication	☐	☐
appropriate vocabulary	☐	☐
body language	☐	☐
social skills	☐	☐

Any comments..

....

c. Communication skills

Writing

Do students have to write:–

	yes	no
memos	☐	☐
notes	☐	☐
discursive essays	☐	☐
narrative essays	☐	☐
descriptive essays	☐	☐
reports	☐	☐
letters	☐	☐
instructions	☐	☐
descriptions of practical work	☐	☐
answers to questions	☐	☐
other		

d. Numerical skills

Do students need to have some knowledge of the following:–

	yes	no
4 rules of number (+ – x ÷)	☐	☐
decimals	☐	☐
fractions	☐	☐
money	☐	☐
weights and measures	☐	☐
percentages	☐	☐
averages	☐	☐
ratio and proportion	☐	☐
area	☐	☐
volume/capacity	☐	☐
time	☐	☐
graphs/tables	☐	☐
use of calculator	☐	☐
algebra	☐	☐
geometry	☐	☐
trigonometry	☐	☐
other		

e. Information Technology

Do students need to have some basic knowledge of I.T.?

Do students need to be aware of:–

	yes	no
use a keyboard	☐	☐
read computer printouts	☐	☐
do word processing	☐	☐
obtain information	☐	☐
other		

Further analysis can then be done on the level of skills required. For example:

- **Are students required to identify the main points from text or interpret what they read and use it to inform a judgement?**

The level of communication and numeracy skills required in particular areas can then be related to the ALBSU Standards Framework to determine the level of basic skills that students are expected to have for that course.

Maximising the effectiveness of teaching methods

Mapping skills in this detailed way helps staff to start to evaluate their teaching methods and course materials to improve access to all students and build in progression during the course.

Analysing a course can also help to focus on areas of difficulty that are commonly experienced by students on that course. Appropriate action can then be considered by both vocational and basic skills staff.

- **Are there a variety of different approaches used that keep the students interested and account for the abilities within the group?**

- **How are the resources used to reinforce learning?**

- **Are students aware of the main points and structure of the lesson at the beginning?**

- **Is student interaction built into the lesson?**

- **Are students expected to reformulate ideas and express them in their own words?**

- **Is students' prior knowledge being activated?**

Maximising the effectiveness of resources used

Course materials, e.g. handouts and text, assignment tasks can be analysed and related to the basic skills levels. Where there is a discrepancy between the level of difficulty of the material, the level required for the course and the level of the student then a re-assessment may need to be undertaken.

- **Is the material above the level of the course?**

- **Would the students benefit more if it was simplified?**

- **Could the materials be differentiated to cope with a variety of abilities within the group?**

- **Have readability factors been taken into account when designing handouts?**

- **Has technical vocabulary been explained to students?**

- **Have new concepts been explained in everyday language with specialist terms introduced gradually?**

Developing vocationally relevant resources

Collaboration between vocational and basic skills staff often results in new material resources designed to develop basic skills within the vocational course and to help students to overcome barriers to success.

In terms of the subject, the basic skills member of staff is in a similar position to the student and can appreciate the basic problems that students are having. The vocational tutor, with their competence and expert knowledge, can find it difficult to identify with problems at this basic level.

Responding to the requirements of different vocational areas requires:

- **a knowledge of the course requirements**
- **a knowledge of the teaching methods**
- **a knowledge of the students.**

How can skills be developed using a variety of material resources?

Analysing the skills involved in reading and understanding instructions resulted in suggestions of the types of exercises that would help students to develop these skills. This type of framework is useful as part of any guidelines devised for resource development and this format can be developed to include an analysis of a whole range of communication and numeracy skills.

SKILLS	SUBSKILLS	EXERCISE TYPES
skimming for overall idea	immediate word recognition fast eye movement ability to use headings and subheadings	comparison of word pairs, wordsearches, jigsaws, cloze passages speed reading exercise matching titles to text, using titles/subtitles to predict, summarising
scanning for details	immediate word recognition fast eye movement ability to search for info using minimal clues	searching for selected words and giving location, cloze exercises, comparison of word pairs, word searches speed reading exercise searching for specific bits of information True or False

SKILLS	SUBSKILLS	EXERCISE TYPES
reading for detail	immediate word recognition finding of relevant info	setting of questions answering self set and teacher set questions – standard, multichoice, looking for irrelevant sentences/words/phrases, separating 2 sets of mixed instructions, rewriting instructions in easier language. True or False, Do's or Don'ts, Right or Wrong
reading for organisation/structure	picking out main points subsidiary points headings/subheadings identifying keywords/points	Flow charts, charts, diagrams – self-made and provided by teacher. Rewriting paragraphs as list of key stages in instruction. Choosing route through options on using flow charts. Matching headings to paragraphs, paragraphs to pictures, recording jumbled text, rewriting in easier language, underlining, making notes, multichoice comprehension.
recognising technical terms/difficult vocabulary understanding technical terms/difficult vocabulary	knowledge of meanings of words knowledge of sentence structures	cloze exercises, multichoice definitions. matching word to definition, labelling diagrams/illustrations matching sentence halves matching paragraphs, sentences, headings to diagrams/illustrations spotting wrong words and sentences inserted rewriting instructions in easier language

In a practical context, these ideas can then be developed as a series of booklets to help, for example, catering and hospitality students to improve their reading skills alongside developing their vocational knowledge.

WORKSHEET 3

1) These paragraphs should have headings. Read very quickly through each paragraph to get a general idea. Then, read them again more slowly and try to match them to the headings. Look up any words which you do not understand.

Headings:-

Heavy Spraycleaning/Light Scrubbing – Ranger Super 400X only

Dry Burnishing   Spraycleaning   Operating Your Machine

Do not Adjust Handle Position with Machine Running

Paragraphs:-

a) With the mains plug connected to the supply, the light on the back of the handle will show that power is being supplied to the machine. Use lever to lower the handle to the operating position. Either left or right On/Off switch levers will operate the machine. Release switch lever and machine will stop.

b) With the brush or pad level on the floor, the machine will stay in a central position. Raise the handle slightly and machine will move to the right. Lower handle slightly and machine will move to the left. Whilst operating the machine, loop the mains cable over shoulder to keep it clear of the machine path.

Always work backwards in open areas, preferably, operating from side to side. Relax whilst operating the machine, it will handle better and will be less fatiguing.

c) Choose the correct pad or brush for the application. Use of the Suction Unit, suction skirt and hose assembly ensures effortless dust control.

d) Use a pad recommended for spraycleaning or a sprayclean brush, dust particles will be contained by use of the Suction Unit, skirt and hose assembly. For best results always use the recommended dilution of spraycleaning solution.

e) With the Solution Unit removed and the Solution Tank and recommended brush or pad fitted. Fill the Solution Tank with the correct dilution of product for the application observing the indicated level. The Solution control lever allows the operator to dispense the required amount of solution through the centre feed for even cleaning.

---

2) You have just shown a new cleaner how to work the machine, but before she starts using it, you want her to tell you how to move it safely. Write down a check list of the points you would expect her to be able to tell you.

....

....

....

....

....

Horticulture students needed to memorise large amounts of information on their course about plants and their Latin names. Helping them to develop strategies for this was a priority.

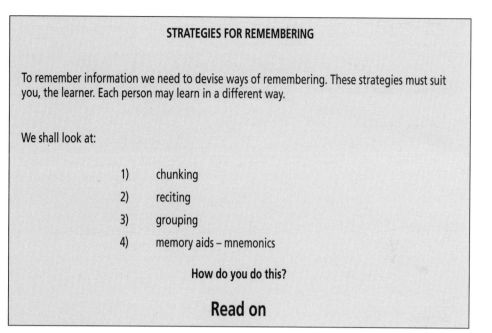

STRATEGIES FOR REMEMBERING

To remember information we need to devise ways of remembering. These strategies must suit you, the learner. Each person may learn in a different way.

We shall look at:

1) chunking

2) reciting

3) grouping

4) memory aids – mnemonics

How do you do this?

Read on

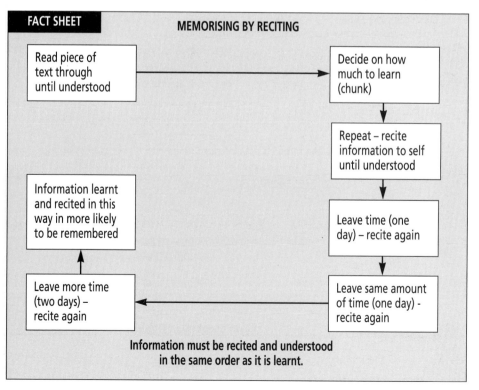

FACT SHEET   **MEMORISING BY RECITING**

Read piece of text through until understood → Decide on how much to learn (chunk)

Repeat – recite information to self until understood

Leave time (one day) – recite again

Leave same amount of time (one day) - recite again

Leave more time (two days) – recite again

Information learnt and recited in this way in more likely to be remembered

**Information must be recited and understood
in the same order as it is learnt.**

In GNVQ Intermediate Art & Design the students had to develop an understanding of the different movements that had influenced the development of Art & Design. They needed a lot of reinforcement work to help them to understand the nature of each movement and to help them to prepare for their end-tests.

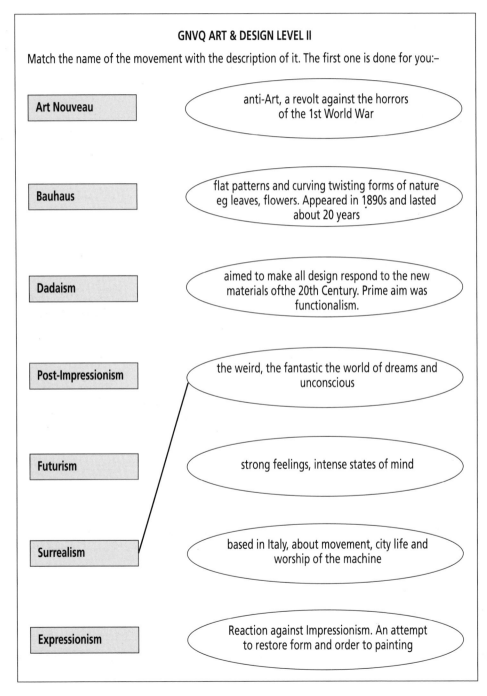

GNVQ ART & DESIGN LEVEL II

Match the name of the movement with the description of it. The first one is done for you:–

Art Nouveau	anti-Art, a revolt against the horrors of the 1st World War
Bauhaus	flat patterns and curving twisting forms of nature eg leaves, flowers. Appeared in 1890s and lasted about 20 years
Dadaism	aimed to make all design respond to the new materials of the 20th Century. Prime aim was functionalism.
Post-Impressionism	the weird, the fantastic the world of dreams and unconscious
Futurism	strong feelings, intense states of mind
Surrealism	based in Italy, about movement, city life and worship of the machine
Expressionism	Reaction against Impressionism. An attempt to restore form and order to painting

There also needed to be ways of checking and developing the students' understanding of terms in Art & Design.

TERMS USED IN ART AND DESIGN

Fill in the missing words:–

1. **Aesthetics** is about principles of _____ and _____.

2. The **Fine Arts** are music, painting, _____ and poetry.

3. **Applied Arts** are arts which are _____ as well as artistic.

4. The **Renaissance** was a _____ of art and ideas in Italy.

5. **Medieval** means _____.

6. **Classical** art is excellent according to a firmly established set of _____.

7. **Romantic** art is the opposite of _____ art.

8. **Romantic** art is free and _____.

9. **Mock** means _____.

10. **Contemporary** means _____.

11. **Symbolism** is about the use of _____ to represent the idea or essence of things.

12. **Figurative** art is _____ and _____.

13. **Non-figurative** art is _____ and _____.

14. A **genre** is a _____ of picture usually of everyday life and portraits.

15. **Texture** is the _____ feel of an object eg rough, smooth.

16. **Naive Art** is _____, innocent art.

17. An example of **Naive Art** is _____.

In Engineering, students were having large chunks of the underpinning knowledge requirements for their course delivered by video. A structured approach was needed to encourage:

- **active listening**

- **an understanding of the key points prior to watching the video**

- **to act as a reinforcement exercise later in the course**

- **give structure to the session that would prompt interaction and discussion.**

ENGINEERING CRAFT STUDIES
Keeping in Place

In this video you will see:

a)   how a piece of work has three degrees of motion at right angles to each other

b)   how the work can be restrained by clamps and stops

c)   methods of restraining work on a lathe

d)   how it is possible to damage work while restraining it.

Watch the **video** and **answer** these **questions:-**

1)   Where is the component restrained on a large industrial lathe?

2)   What happens if you drill components which are not properly restrained?

3)   What could happen to the component when using a grindwheel?

4)   A component which has no movement in all three directions is:

_____   _____ .

5)   Where are drills mounted on a lathe?

6)   To centre a component, which drill do you use **first** _____ ,
       second _____ .

7)   How would you provide restraint in the downward direction?

8)   What is a vice?

9)   How would you restrain a **round** component?

10)   Can you use a magnetic V block to restrain any material?

11)   How can a round component be restrained on a lathe?

12)   What happens to a rod if the V blocks are placed too far apart?

13)   When would you used a fixed steady?

14)   When should packing pieces be used?

Skills Mapping Tasks

As well as skills mapping courses, skills mapping tasks and assignments can also help tutors and students to identify where the areas of difficulty might arise.

This assignment was used in the 'Language of Dance' option for the BTEC National Diploma in Performing Arts Year 2.

BTEC NATIONAL DIPLOMA IN PERFORMING ARTS　　　　　　**LANGUAGE OF DANCE II**

Instructions to Students

Research your chosen choreographer. Look at the historical background which has produced his/her style of choreography.

Notice any recurring styles of choreography, design, etc, and any deviations from his/her usual style.

Analyse one piece of choreography fully in your written project and produce an abridged version for your demonstration, selecting the important elements you wish to communicate.

Assessment

50% Lecture demonstration　　　50% Written project.

BTEC NATIONAL DIPLOMA IN PERFORMING ARTS　　　　　　**LANGUAGE OF DANCE II**

Assignment Outline

To present a lecture demonstration and written project on a given choreographer.

(i) The lecture demonstration will include historical details and a brief analysis of one piece of his/her choreography.

(ii) The written project will include visual information, social and historical background and a written analysis of the one piece of choreography chosen in (i).

Assessment

50% Lecture demonstration　　　50% Written project.

Objectives

(a) Recognise and place specific dance works in their historical context.

(b) Demonstrate an understanding of 20th Century dance.

(c) Evaluate the working relationship between the elements involved in performance, music, design and choreography.

The skills in the assignment were mapped.

LANGUAGE OF DANCE II   **Choreographer Assignment**

Part 1

Research skills

Reading skills   – skimming

                     – scanning   }   variety of texts – textbooks, trade journals, leaflets

                     – effective reading

Note-taking   – from tutor's introduction

                     – video

                     – written sources

Ordering of information into chronological sequencing

From written information   – chronological order – biographical piece

                                    – analysis – necessary to understand subject specific vocabulary

Appropriate spelling, punctuation, grammar, syntax

Part 2

Summarising. Main points from Part 1 for Oral Presentation

Provide information clearly and in sensible order

Present opinions clearly and concisely

Provide sensible supporting arguments for opinions presented

Use appropriate volume, tone of voice, articulation and body language

Use visual aids effectively   – pictures, blow-ups

                               – video (to demonstrate points in analysis)

Effective use of cue-cards rather than reading out from a script

---

The vocational lecturer had noted in the past that:

"The Students displayed poor time management skills – they didn't realise that there was so much to do. There was not enough research and their analysis was poor. They described the dance, but didn't explain what was going on – eg different types of movement, describing motifs etc. They need to develop the correct balance between 50% analysis/presentation and 50% written work."

Solution:

- **To produce a more detailed dance analysis plan and list of key terms involved in analysis**
- **To do some work on time management**
- **To revise research skills.**

Building a partnership between vocational lecturers and basic skills lecturers

Vocational staff need to understand the role of the basic skills lecturer and how they can fit into the vocational area.

To work effectively, this kind of partnership needs to be developed in a constructive way. The basic skills lecturer is not there to tell the vocational lecturer what is wrong with their delivery style! There also needs to be a positive direction to it in terms of a clearly defined role for each participating member of staff or course team and some expected outcomes.

On-course support produces tangible outcomes in terms of:

- **increase in staff expertise, confidence and skills**

- **imaginative course structures and delivery methods that are student centred**

- **materials that can be used and developed in more than one setting**

- **the development of basic skills in a vocationally relevant context.**

Each vocational area will have different requirements. The success of the work depends on being sensitive to these and producing a plan that benefits both staff and students.

Working in this way helps vocational staff to incorporate strategies for developing students' basic skills into their teaching, thus reducing the need for regular input from basic skills staff.

Overleaf are some of the ways that support work has developed in different vocational areas.

Informing workshop staff

The information gained by basic skills staff of particular vocational areas can inform other workshop staff in a number of ways:

- **information about course content and structure and the basic skills that students need can be fed back into the workshop and inform the assessment procedure**

- **course profiles can be built up in a systematic way and developed into self assessment checklists for students**

- **information about student need and course requirements can influence the development and purchase of workshop materials.**

DEVELOPMENT OF SUPPORT WORK WITHIN IN THE MOTOR VEHICLE SECTOR

Meeting with Senior Lecturer

↓

Screening of Students

↓

Informal liaison with individual members of staff

↓

Observation of classes →	Vocational checklist completed
Familiarity of course content →	Discussion of resources needed
Identify demands on students	

End of Term 1

↓

Production of short series of handouts on Preparing for your Practical Assessments, Summarising Information from Car Manuals and Writing a Short Report

↓

Disseminated to other members of staff by vocational lecturer and added to materials bank

↓

Meeting with Training Provider at the request of the Senior Lecturer to discuss development of basic skills

↓

Extra funding secured from TEC. A short module for six students run at English Workshop on main site for six weeks on Effective Reading and Note-taking

Terms 2 & 3

↓

Booklet of materials produced to support students on Industrial Studies Module

↓

Short inputs on planning, structuring and presentation given by basic skills tutor team teaching with vocational staff coupled with individual help on sentence structure and spelling

↓

Strategies discussed and evaluated by vocational staff. Ways of incorporating these into other parts of the course considered.

↓

——— BY THE END OF YEAR ONE ———

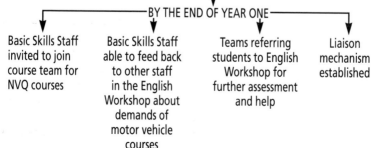

Basic Skills Staff invited to join course team for NVQ courses	Basic Skills Staff able to feed back to other staff in the English Workshop about demands of motor vehicle courses	Teams referring students to English Workshop for further assessment and help	Liaison mechanism established

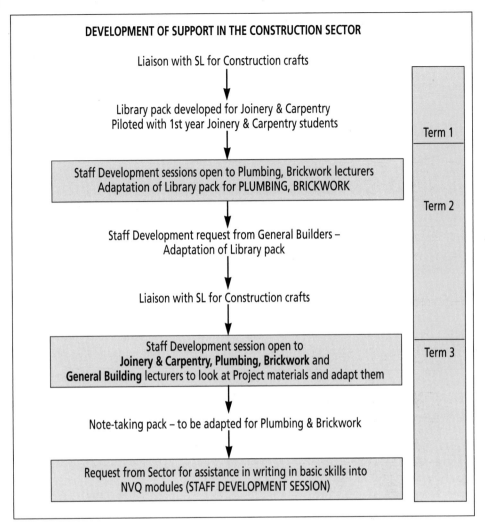

DEVELOPMENT OF SUPPORT IN THE CONSTRUCTION SECTOR

Liaison with SL for Construction crafts

↓

Library pack developed for Joinery & Carpentry
Piloted with 1st year Joinery & Carpentry students

↓

Staff Development sessions open to Plumbing, Brickwork lecturers
Adaptation of Library pack for PLUMBING, BRICKWORK

↓

Staff Development request from General Builders –
Adaptation of Library pack

↓

Liaison with SL for Construction crafts

↓

Staff Development session open to
Joinery & Carpentry, Plumbing, Brickwork and
General Building lecturers to look at Project materials and adapt them

↓

Note-taking pack – to be adapted for Plumbing & Brickwork

↓

Request from Sector for assistance in writing in basic skills into
NVQ modules (STAFF DEVELOPMENT SESSION)

Term 1

Term 2

Term 3

- **workshop tutors can make the work given to students more vocationally relevant from a background of increased knowledge**
- **the pooling of strategies and ideas by workshop staff working in vocational areas can ensure that consistent good practice is developed throughout the College.**

Working in this kind of flexible way, responding to the needs of all staff for professional development and a supportive framework within which to evaluate and develop good practice, benefits all students. By extending the skills of vocational and basic skills support staff, the students can progress within a well planned course where their individual needs are recognised and addressed. A student support system cannot rely solely on the skills of specialist staff when there are many improvements that can be made on courses by course teams that will help to remove some of the barriers that students face during their time in college.

8 | *Conclusion*

Basic skills support work can affect all areas of the curriculum across a variety of levels. It is clearly a flexible provision that aims to identify and respond to the needs of students and staff and to influence course development.

This examination of the different aspects of basic skills support reveals a number of issues that need to be explored and resolved by colleges. This will involve people with a variety of roles working in all contexts within a college.

Senior Managers will need to devise policies that support the identification and development of students' basic skills. They will also need to ensure that these policies are implemented and supported by structures within the college. It will include access to staff development opportunities as well as a management structure that facilitates the planning of provision. Senior Managers will be responsible for identifying sources of funding for the development of this work, principally through the Further Education Funding Council.

Coordinators and Middle Managers, as part of their role, will have to set up systems that monitor and evaluate this support at all levels to ensure that it is efficient in its operation and effective in providing help to those students who most need it. This will involve the allocating of available resources in a way that maximises their potential; the planning of future development; the support and direction of staff; securing realistic resource levels that reflect the evidence of need and devising 'user friendly' systems for both staff and students.

Basic Skills Staff will need to be prepared to learn about the demands of different vocational areas and translate these into practical help for students and staff. They will have to adapt materials and strategies to suit the vocational context and be prepared to work in a flexible way. Liaison and the building of trust and confidence with both staff and students will be of the utmost importance and they will need the ability to identify and take advantage of opportunities as they arise.

Vocational Staff will have a vital role in supporting students development not only in their vocational skills but in their communication and numeracy skills. Taking a fresh look at courses and their materials and delivery methods can reap dividends for both staff and students in the long run. It may seem initially that this is yet 'just another demand' on staff who are already over-stretched and under pressure. A partnership with basic skills staff can help to give new insights into reasons for some students' lack of progress and look at practical ways of addressing this. Recognising the part that they have to play in removing barriers to progression within a course, and identifying when specialist help is required for individuals or groups of students, will help to bring about the fundamental changes that are required.

The Future

Colleges are at varying stages in their development of basic skills support work. Those who are just starting to develop this kind of work can learn from the experience of colleges who have more expertise in the area. All colleges, whatever stage they have reached in developing support, will need to continue to refine and progress their provision in certain key areas.

These are:

- **developing individualised approaches with students as a way of providing relevant learning programmes**

- **devising systems for tracking students and measuring their learning gain to look at how support has enhanced their progress**

- **liaising more closely with local schools to improve the quality of information about students' abilities on entering further education**

- **improving information for the initial advice and guidance of students**

- **measuring the effectiveness of basic skills support in terms of student confidence, skill development, retention and achievement**

- **increasing the use of new technology in basic skills support**

- **incorporating basic skills materials into Resource Based Learning facilities**

- **looking at techniques that support students in taking more responsibility for their learning**

- **continuing to examine the role of screening, the best time to carry it out and which methods of screening and assessment to use**

- **securing adequate funding to support basic skills development for those students who need it.**

This consideration of basic skills in the wider context of other developments ensures that it is accepted as an integral part of college activity and is not marginalised or seen as a service for a minority of students.

The broader aims of further education are to prepare students for other education and training opportunities or their working life, in addition to the primary aim of helping them to achieve on their college programmes. Basic skills are a key to an individual's success and provide a foundation for future progress and development and students are entitled to expect that these will be developed alongside their vocational skills in their time in college. The cost of ignoring basic skills has been far too high for both institutions and individuals.

Supporting students in the development of these skills, even at this comparatively late stage in their education, will pay dividends for the long term economic prosperity of the country and help individuals to realise their potential.

Bibliography

General Background Reading:

Audit Commission, *Unfinished Business: Full-time educational courses for young people aged 16-19* - HMSO

Bynner J. EkinSmyth C., *The Basic Skills of Young Adults* - ALBSU

Fletcher S., *NVQs - Standards and Competence* - Kogan Page

Mobley M., *Evaluating Curriculum Materials*

Rowntree D., *Assessing Students: How shall we know them?* - Kogan Page

Rye J., *Cloze Procedure and the Teaching of Reading* - Heinemann Educational Books

Recurrent Funding for 1994-95: Guidance to Institutions. Circular 93/39 - FEFC

Core Skills Action Pack: Principles for the development of core skills across the curriculum - FEU

Assessment Issues and Problems in an Criterion-Based System - FEU

The Cost to Industry Basic Skills and the UK Workforce - ALBSU

Basic Skills Support in Colleges: Assessing the Need - ALBSU

Specific publications that are helpful for basic skills teaching and learning:

Brittan J., *An Introduction to Numeracy Teaching* - ALBSU

Gittins R., *An Introduction to Literacy Teaching* - ALBSU

Gordon T., *Working with Language - A guide for Vocational Trainers with Bilingual Trainees* - NFER

Jordan J., *An Introdcution to ESOL Teaching* - ALBSU

Klein C., *Diagnosing Dyslexia - A Guide to the Assessment of Adults with Specific Learning Difficulties* - ALBSU

Leonard J., *Wordprocessing and Language Skills* - ALBSU

Smith A., *Language Guidelines - Developing reading, writing and oral skills across the curriculum* - Hodder & Stoughton

Viewpoints No 12 Basic Skills in Further Education - ALBSU

Working Together - An Approach to Functional Literacy - ALBSU

Basic Skills Software Guide - ALBSU

Assessing Reading and Maths - A Screening Test - ALBSU

Basic Skills Assessment - ALBSU

The ALBSU Standards for Basic Skills Students and Trainees - ALBSU

The ALBSU Standards for Basic Skills Teachers - ALBSU

Wallcharts: Mapping the ALBSU Standards to GNVQ Core Skills in Communication and the Application of Number - ALBSU

Individuality in Learning - A guide to understanding and promoting individual learning - FEU

Index